Behaviour at Work

Christopher E. Stafford

Senior Lecturer in Business and Management Studies
Plymouth College of Further Education

CAMBRIDGE
UNIVERSITY PRESS

Published by the Press Syndicate of the University of Cambridge
The Pitt Building, Trumpington Street, Cambridge CB2 1RP
40 West 20th Street, New York, NY 10011-4211, USA
10 Stamford Road, Oakleigh, Melbourne 3166, Australia

First published 1994

Printed in Great Britain by Scotprint Ltd, Musselburgh

A catalogue record for this book is available from the British Library

ISBN 0 521 47851 0 paperback

Cover illustration by Gary Thompson

Contents

Preface

To the tutor 'The success or failure of a business within a given marketplace depends on the organisation's success in using its resources.'

Behaviour at Work is about business organisations and their major resource – people. It has been specifically written to give students working for GNVQ Advanced Business a user-friendly text which fully covers the Unit Specification and enables them to be involved in a range of activities and tasks designed to provide a comprehensive formative and summative assessment strategy.

The quotation above from the rationale for this Unit is very simple, but it has a wide range of implications for any business organisation. One of the most important is that an organisation is a *dynamic* entity which is developing and changing all the time, and the text is structured initially to reinforce this concept, using an innovative approach to introduce the student to a variety of ideas, and two challenging case studies. Although they come relatively early in the programme, these case studies are recommended as formal assessments because they encourage students to gain breadth of understanding in the context of organisations with which they can readily identify, and give tutors the scope to lead and manage learning through discussions and analysis of *real* situations. From this broad introduction the student is led into a carefully structured consideration of the concepts specified in the performance criteria across the range, and is required to demonstrate practical application of knowledge to both personal and case study situations. The balance of theory and practice demands standards appropriate to a course at this advanced level.

This text is ideal for use in student-centred learning environments, or as a comprehensive back-up to a tutor-led approach. It manages the student's learning through a logical development of themes linked to relevant assessment activities, and provides a medium through which the on-going development and testing of core skills can be achieved. The material has been tried and tested in the classroom by experienced tutors, and its recognised success is in providing a practical and demanding work programme for students through a learning process that balances academic rigour and the realistic application of knowledge in a vocational context.

As well as specifically covering the Behaviour at Work Option Unit for GNVQ Advanced Business, tutors will find that it is a useful core reference source for many Management courses, providing coverage of a wide range of objectives across a number of units for students who need to draw on a variety of learning resources during their programme.

Assessments and activities There are six main assessments in the text, which provide the focus of assessment for this GNVQ Unit. These are supported by a wide range of activities designed to reinforce essential knowledge and skills. This gives tutors the flexibility to select a balance of activities that are appropriate to the needs/resources of their students and yet provide a coherent and on-going assessment programme.

To the student The general themes you will consider as part of this GNVQ Unit revolve around the following elements:

- the factors influencing attitudes and performance at work (including the dynamic and constantly changing nature of work)

- groups at work

- the behavioural aspects of managing people which influence performance at work.

This might not, at first glance, seem very much to deal with, but there are many complex concepts to grasp, and practical assignments in which you are expected to apply your knowledge and understanding.

You will find that the material is divided into four main sections, each of which is intended to develop or support certain ideas embodied in the GNVQ Unit Specification. The units within each section of this book pinpoint specific aspects of the overall theme, and contain the basic knowledge you require, together with a series of activities and assessments. These activities and assessments form an on-going assessment strategy, with a balance of knowledge reinforcement exercises, real case studies, investigations, research, and analyses of personal experience. All the work you do during the year will contribute towards your final grades, with the six main assignments providing the focus.

The content As a broad introduction to some of the general influences on organisation activities, Section One (Units 1–4) looks at why an organisation has to be dynamic, what effects this can have on individuals and groups, and how – in general terms – an effective management strategy can encourage positive attitudes and behaviour. An appreciation of this background of perpetual change is essential to an understanding of how the complexities of human relations and behavioural principles can create an effective (or ineffective) working environment.

Section Two (Units 5–8) is concerned with the way in which people behave and interact through the formation of groups and teams. You will start with a basic appreciation of how individual attitudes are formed and how various influences contribute to the development and evolution of that individual, and then move on to consider why people join groups, and the dynamics of group operation. There are brief case studies, activities and assessments to reinforce your understanding, and an important unit on the group as a 'team'.

A natural progression from this work is to look at the operation of groups and individuals from the point of view of a manager, and to analyse the skills and qualities needed by any individual who takes on a leadership role in an organisation. Links between leadership and management are considered, and the concept of effective communication as an essential characteristic of good management is looked at in some detail. The emphasis all the time is on people, human relations, and behaviour, and this forms the link between Section Three (Units 9–11) and Section Four (Units 12–15), showing how people fit into and react within a range of organisational structures and how they contribute to and adapt to organisational cultures. This leads us into the complex areas of motivation, job satisfaction, job design and quality control as the final topics for you to think about in your study of *Behaviour at Work*.

The dynamic organisation

About Section One The concept of 'dynamic development' is really a theme which is relevant to, and runs through the whole of your study and assessment programme. However, in order to appreciate the significance of the concept in the context of business and the work environment, it is important for you to have a balance of theoretical ideas, practical examples, and relevant background material. Therefore you are not asked specifically to relate the ideas to a particular business, but are given the opportunity to broaden your appreciation of how such constant change can affect the business world in general, and the society in which we live.

The delivery of these units revolves around a progressive introduction to the ideas, starting with some basic theory. It consists of a number of readings and a range of activities designed to test your knowledge and assess your understanding. You will find some of the readings quite difficult and others fairly easy, and the variety of tasks you are asked to do range from straightforward 'comprehension-type' questions to consideration of case studies. The first two written activities will involve answering questions which should help you grasp some of the basic ideas and implications. In order to develop further ideas the main assessments give you the opportunity to study and analyse real case studies.

Unit 1

The background – a 'dynamic' society

Reading 1   In recent years, the economic and business environment has become much more turbulent, uncertain and demanding. Politicians and business leaders tell us that we are in 'an era of unprecedented change' and 'predictability is a thing of the past'. We can identify a number of areas in which change has taken place:

- Economic and political change has led to a rise in recent years of the enterprise culture and an emphasis on the market economy.

- Changes in social attitudes have produced a tendency towards individual rather than community or national achievement.

- The expectations of consumers are higher than ever before, demanding not only value for money but also higher standards of quality and service.

- The business community is having to make significant changes because of increased competition from Europe, other producers, multinational firms, and the pressures of an unstable economy.

- Firms must innovate to remain competitive and to establish and maintain their position in markets, because product life cycles are shorter and the consumer is always looking for something 'better'.

- New technology is playing a much greater part in all aspects of business, from production to management information systems.

Reading 2   Change is inevitable in any organisation – even those regarded as static or stable: it simply means that change in them is gradual rather than non-existent. Change is brought about by many different influences, and some of these are discussed in the following paragraphs.

   Most governments adopt the attitude that a monopoly situation does not create a healthy business environment, and the fact that there are very few companies that would claim to offer a unique product or service means that the majority operate in a competitive market. Competition from other companies means that it is important to monitor what is going on in the particular industry – especially if a competitor is about to launch a new product or mount a new advertising campaign. Change will be a constant and dynamic process if a company is to keep ahead of the competition, and in large companies the Research and Development Department is a vital component of success.

In our modern world, products rapidly become out of date, fashions change, and the consequent changes in consumer demand mean that organisations have to change in order to survive. Catalytic converters, turbo chargers, CDs and microwave ovens, for example, have become 'fashionable' products in recent years, together with low-calorie and low-alcohol drinks. We demand different services such as the facility for 'one-stop' shopping – hence the demise of the corner shop; we don't want to bother with returning bottles, so there is the disposable plastic or cardboard container; if our conscience pricks us we look towards recyclable packaging, and this then becomes a 'selling point' or 'advantage' of a particular brand product; advances in technology mean that we have grown to demand more facilities in the home, and computers form an essential part of our lives – for work, entertainment, teaching/learning, information services, communication links, and even shopping. All such developments mean that companies that can adapt to meet the demands will expand rapidly, and those that can't will go into decline. The name of the game in business is to anticipate impending changes and *act*.

New products and new technology can have a dramatic impact on an organisation, ranging from a complete review of production processes and the re-design of jobs, to adjustment in hours worked and even a significant shift in the proportion of white-collar to blue-collar workers. Such *innovation* can be seen in many different areas – see those in Figure 1, for example.

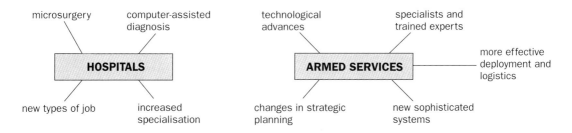

Figure 1   Innovation with an organisation

The *workforce* will always be at the centre of any change, and in reality it is a constant source of change for any organisation. People join and leave, are promoted or transferred, are re-trained and develop new skills. Even before employment, we can see the way in which education and training has developed over the last few decades: a different and longer education process has been introduced; there has been a move away from traditional rote learning towards a discovery-based approach designed to improve under-standing and encourage analytical thought. As a consequence the intellectual capabilities of the workforce have increased significant-ly, and this in turn means that management techniques have had to change, and the work environment (Herzberg's 'hygiene' factor – see Unit 13) have been improved. Trade unions have played an important role in our economic lives, but as we have seen in recent years, this influence is constantly fluctuating – sometimes very strong, but diminishing rapidly in times of economic depression and high unemployment.

Tied in closely with improvements in education and training is the movement that has occurred in social values and attitudes, the trend towards more ecological awareness being one of the most sig-nificant. Some examples are shown in Figure 2.

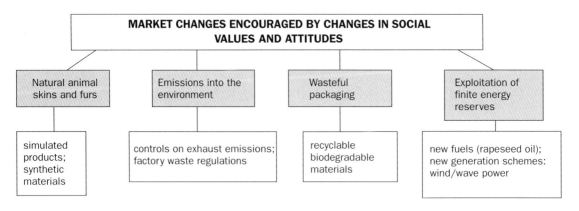

Figure 2   Some recent changes in social values and attitudes

In the background is always *government.* In fact it has been more and more in the foreground in recent times, with an increasing level of intervention in the running of industry (overt or covert). On the positive side there has been much legislation designed to improve

Wind farms – sources of renewable energy – are visible evidence of the change in social attitudes relating to energy use

the quality of working life, ranging from health and safety at work to equal pay, equal opportunities and anti-discrimination. Recruitment, selection, redundancy and dismissal are all aspects of employment which have received attention and have had an effect on the way organisations treat their staff. In the financial sector a plethora of regulations and controls have been introduced, creating the need for more specialists with different skills.

Reading 3   In our constantly changing world, few things are unchanging. This is partly the result of rapidly advancing technology, and partly the result of natural processes. Oil is discovered by an ailing country, and a declining economy suddenly 'takes off', until the resource is used up or a cheaper substitute is found. The birth rate falls, and the demand for baby-related products declines. A celebrity appears on television wearing a baseball cap back to front and suddenly everyone is walking around looking like the back end of a duck-billed platypus. As a result of purely natural forces, our coastline changes its shape through erosion, continents 'drift' and the universe evolves.

Reading 4   With constant progress and the introduction of new methods of working, organisations must adapt to ensure that they can maintain their market positions or continue to provide the service the public wants in the most efficient way. 'Change' is a continuous process, but it does not only relate to ideas, concepts, systems and methods – it also relates to people. Without people organisations would not exist and nothing would get done. Therefore if the people who are responsible for running modern business do not receive the necessary education, training, knowledge and support, the new systems cannot work effectively, and essential developments cannot be implemented.

As change is inevitable in any organisation, it is worth considering where the pressure for change comes from. Figure 3 outlines some influences on and aspects of change, ranging from specific work-practices to general attitudes in society. These are not intended to be comprehensive or exclusive but aim to give a general awareness and overview of the way in which society, education, government, industry and commerce interact to create and affect our working environment.

Competition	<ul><li>constant monitoring of what other companies offer</li><li>matching and improving on competitors' products</li><li>on-going research and development</li></ul>
Changes in consumer wants	<ul><li>products quickly become 'dated' – consumers want the newest</li><li>fashion demands rapid change</li><li>changes in shopping patterns, presentation and packaging of goods</li><li>consumer power can lead to decline for companies who have not foreseen changes</li></ul>
New products new technology	<ul><li>automation, robotics – direct effects on job design, manpower, hours, etc</li><li>requirement for new skills, different technology, investment</li><li>effective training programmes are essential</li></ul>
The government	<ul><li>legislation relating to working conditions and employment</li><li>financial regulations and control</li><li>market conditions monitored, take-overs controlled, monopolies scrutinised</li></ul>
The workforce	<ul><li>improvements in education and training</li><li>changes in management styles – participative management</li><li>the role of trade unions – consultation, negotiation</li></ul>
Society	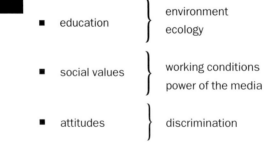

Figure 3 Some influences on and aspects of change

Activity 1

You should produce written answers to these *after* considering the preceding readings carefully. If appropriate it could be useful to support your reading by discussion with your tutors.

1 What do you understand by the terms 'enterprise culture' and the 'market economy'?

2 Describe an example of how consumer pressure/attitudes have led to the production of a new product.

3 Why is a *monopoly* regarded as undesirable? How does competition instigate change?

4 Give some examples of how ecological awareness and changes in social values have brought about changes in consumer products.

5 How can management styles or trade union activities contribute *positively* towards change?

Unit 2

From technology to training

One of the most fundamental changes affecting organisations and the way they function is the increased use of information technology, based on advanced computers. Today, miniaturisation of the integrated circuit upon which computers rely, means that the capacity of older equipment (large enough to fill a room) is now equalled by desk-top machines. Moreover, the greatly reduced size of computers and the efficient production of silicon chips (containing the circuit) has allowed prices which make computers widely accessible. For evidence of the growth of computer ownership you need only note that a larger proportion of homes in the UK have computers than in any other country.

Reading 1 We can see the impact of computers in a variety of work situations, ranging from the car production plant to the office. On a car assembly line many of the repetitive tasks like the fitting of basic components, spot welding body panels and painting the body shell are now done using robotics – replacing the human element with a tireless, accurately programmed robot. In the office, the computer is now all-powerful, and many businesses grind to a halt if there is a breakdown, or – even worse – a destructive virus in the system. Storage and retrieval of information, direct mail, accounting procedures, and many complex aspects of management information systems are now totally dependent upon the most modern technology.

One area in which the technological revolution has had the most dramatic effects is the newspaper industry. Gone are the days when the journalists used to type their copy, and pass it to the specialists who would hand-set each letter in metal for every article. No longer do photographs have to go through a lengthy and complex process; nor does each item on a page have to be composed on a semi-cylindrical metal plate which was attached to a roller on the cumbersome printing press. Technology has changed all this. Now the journalist feeds the work into a computer, the computer sets the type and produces the printing plate, photographs are added, and a computer-controlled printer rolls off copies in their thousands. Editing and quality control are made much easier, and the whole process is speeded up.

But what has happened to all those workers who used to be involved in the process? There has been much unrest and conflict over this issue because the disappearance of many of the skilled but time-consuming manual tasks has meant that new working practices and manning levels have had to be introduced. Disputes with the unions became so bitter and protracted that a number of newspaper proprietors decided to move out of the traditional Fleet Street home of the industry, and set up in other areas where financial inducements and advantageous conditions were being offered to attract new industry (eg Enterprise Zones). *The Times* moved to Wapping; *The Daily Telegraph* considered London's Dockland; the *Mirror* group went to Watford.

Another example of the technology revolution can be found in our local supermarkets, but we are probably so used to the bar code system by now that we don't really think of it as being high-tech. How wrong this is! The simple bar code is read by a laser scanner at the checkout, and a number of operations automatically begin: the item is recorded, the quantity and cost are registered, the fact that an item has been sold is entered in the stores stock-control system, monitoring of the stock levels takes place and automatic re-ordering ensures that your favourite product is always on the shelves. The cash till lists, prices and totals everything you have bought so that you have a complete checklist of your day's shopping.

Staying with retailing, cashless transactions are now commonplace using an EFTPOS (electronic funds transfer at point of sale) system. The customer's plastic card is fed through the computer, and instructions are immediately issued to his or her bank or building society to debit the account and transfer the appropriate funds into the supermarket's account. An example of this is the Switch card.

Obviously, the same principles could be applied to combined television/computer installations in the home, and the scope of home-based, cashless shopping becomes enormous.

Bar code laser readers are now a familiar sight at the supermarket checkout

The rapid transfer of information facilitated by the technology revolution has opened up national and international markets, and the sector in which this is most obvious in the worldwide market is in company shares, currencies and commodities. Since the 'Big Bang' on 27 October 1986, and the introduction of SEAQ (Stock Exchange Automated Quotation system), face-to-face dealing on the floor of the Exchange has been replaced, and full facilities for dealing are available at the touch of a button (or key).

It is fairly clear that the introduction of technology into any industry can have repercussions: some jobs are lost; new jobs are created; new procedures and processes necessitate effective education and training programmes. The increased capacity and pervasive use of data processing and information storage systems mean that protective legislation has had to be introduced with Computer Software Copyright Acts and the Data Protection Act.

Reading 2   Very often, it is people's attitudes towards change that cause difficulties in implementation, and the introduction of new technology is one area where reactions are often strongest. In the work environment, a manager often comes up against entrenched attitudes (prejudices) and ideas when he or she wants to introduce a new working practice or change long-standing procedures; and if such changes are imposed, it is often the people at *supervisory* level who have to bear the brunt of any reaction.

As far as technology is concerned, we know that it is one of the important developments in modern business. We also know that attitudes affect people's behaviour, and that influences on the formation of *attitudes* include experience and group membership.

Let us now link these by examining some of the experiences people may have of new technology and some of the views that are expressed concerning the likely impact of technology on patterns of employment, to establish the likely impact on employee attitudes in the future.

It is clear from the current economic climate, that in Britain and most other industrialised countries full employment is an unattainable aim. We cannot expect that all people will be able to be in fulltime employment for the whole of their lives. Some people blame the introduction of new technology for this fact, claiming that machines, computers and robots are doing many things that would previously have required people, and pointing out that not enough new jobs are being created to make up the loss.

However, it would be wrong to put all the blame on new technology. Other factors are equally important. There have been demographic changes and changes in employment patterns which all contribute to the problem. There are many more people wishing to enter and stay in the labour force; many more women now want to continue or return to work when their family commitments allow it; thus the decline in jobs combined with the increase in the labour 'pool' has exacerbated the situation.

Stopping progress by stopping the introduction of new technology is rather a regressive step, so we can look at other ways of manipulating the labour market. One move could be to *reduce the demand* for jobs, but this type of policy would need to be implemented nationally (ie government action) rather than unilaterally by individual firms. What options could be available in this context?

One possibility is that young people could be encouraged (or required) to stay in full-time education or training after the age of 16. This would bring us much more in line with some of our industrialised neighbours – for example, in Germany only 6% of young people leave school without any qualification; in Britain it has been nearer 40%. Additional education and training could usefully be provided in order to raise the skills level of our prospective workforce, and develop some of the new skills demanded by the technological revolution. Thus we could meet two major needs: provide a more skilled workforce, and lower the overall demand for jobs.

Another possible approach is through job-sharing, where one person does part of a job, and the other part(s) is (are) done by someone else. This could provide useful, satisfying and paid employment for more people in an environment where it is impossible to guarantee a full-time job for everyone. Also, many people would actually *prefer* to have good part-time employment, and even though the total number of jobs wouldn't increase, the number of people in employment would. This principle could be applied to many sectors of society – not only married women with families, but also older people of either sex who might welcome the idea of 'phased' retirement, giving them more time to follow their hobbies and interests.

Some employers argue that job-sharing increases the administrative burden on a firm, but it cannot be beyond the scope of government to simplify the administrative systems and requirements in order to get more people into employment.

A similar type of proposal would be to shorten the working hours that make up an average working week. Reducing the norm to, say, 35 hours per week, and removing systematic overtime, would open the doors to creating more jobs. The 'down side' to this idea is that individual employees would certainly have to accept a certain reduction in income, but it may still be a reasonably practical way of lessening the gap between those who want work and the number of jobs available.

We already have a substantial increase in the 'early retirement' policies adopted by many companies, but there may be scope for formalising this, and reducing the statutory retirement age to 60 or even 55. Some claim that this would be prohibitively expensive in terms of pensions etc, but this must be balanced against the costs of large-scale unemployment. A long-term view would be necessary to incorporate forward planning and proper financing of such a move through more flexible pension schemes, tax incentives and other financial measures. Rather than dismissing ideas like this on grounds of cost, we should *plan* for it and thus achieve our ends.

Reading 3   Future patterns of work will be dramatically affected by new technology, and we must all change our attitudes and approaches if the transition is not to be too painful.

The level of skill demanded from workers will rise considerably as traditional manual and unskilled jobs disappear. Therefore an essential ingredient of the 'employment mix' is an effective training and re-training programme which will enable new entrants and existing workers to develop the necessary skills for on-going employment. At the same time as manual jobs decrease and manufacturing/production becomes more automated, opportunities might open up in other areas – particularly the tertiary sector where a main area of growth is in the leisure industry.

Technological change is with us – it is not going to go away. In fact, the pace is likely to increase (note the massive changes in the service industries such as banking and insurance). Young people should be encouraged to think of their working lives as a series of careers, not just one job. Changing opportunities will require them to take advantage of the chances that come their way – they will need to be adaptable, forward looking, and willing to re-train two or three times in a lifetime. There are many positive sides to current trends and it will require positive and dynamic attitudes to make the best of them.

The future will be tough, and we must create a society to match.

Activity 2   Produce written answers to the following questions, aiming to write a
paragraph on each. You may wish to discuss the topics in class or in small
groups in order to clarify your ideas; or, if you are working at home, try out
some of your ideas and thoughts on a friend or family member who can
discuss the issues with you.

1   How would you describe current employment trends? What influences
are affecting them?

2   How could the following concepts be applied to improve the employment situation:
  – training
  – job sharing.

3   What moves could governments make to enable some of the ideas
outlined in Reading 2 of this unit to be implemented?

Reading 4   What encouraging possibilities does new technology open up for us
in working patterns and relationships? Figure 4 overleaf gives us
some ideas to think about.

   On the industrial relations front, the introduction of new technology can provide the catalyst for a new era of negotiation and co-
operation. Agreements on working practices and implementation
will be negotiated and with improved information/communication
procedures more positive attitudes will be encouraged and feelings
of uncertainty counteracted. There will be scope for developments
in the fields of training, re-training, new salary structures, working
conditions and security of employment. All in all, an effective strategy of implementation through consultation should provide a
potential for more favourable attitudes amongst a workforce.

   What about the organisation itself? New technology often provides the impetus for organisational change in terms of structure.
As new working methods are introduced there might be a movement away from traditional, functional-based structures towards a
product-based or matrix structure, thus bringing more opportunity
for autonomy, team working, responsibility, decision making, more
challenging work – that is, generally improving the quality of working life for employees.

a Job satisfaction		
	The demand for specialist skills	new job more interesting
		new job more fulfilling
		new job more motivating
	Increased opportunities for team or group work	co-operation with others
		common goals
		work-support systems

b Participation		
	Planning	group autonomy
		co-ordination
		identifying goals/objectives
		improved productivity
	Decision making	consultation
		co-operation
		discussion
		improved industrial relations
	Quality management	total quality management (TQM)
		quality circles
		regular consultation
		corporate goals

c Alternative work methods		
	Homeworking or Networking	linked computer terminals mean people can work from home
		flexibility of work times, as long as the work is done
		accommodates working mothers more easily
		saves travel
		can make employment of the disabled easier

Figure 4   How new technology affects work patterns and relationships

Assessment One   The readings in this technology unit make it clear that effective training is an essential part of introducing changes into the work environment. A later unit deals in more detail with strategies for the implementation of change, but it is time for us to look at a real situation and consider a real case study in order to help you see how the theory applies to the business world.

This case study shows how a major retailing organisation, Asda, combined its recognition of the need for a 'European outlook' with a wide-ranging training programme. As you will see, this is no normal in-house training scheme.

The case study does not deal with 'technology' as such, but introduces you to much wider principles, and broader organisational aims. It is easy to grasp the fact that if you introduce a new system or computerised process into a company, someone will have to be trained to operate it. It is much more difficult to think in terms of overall company aims and policy, and see how diverse aspects of an organisation need to be co-ordinated in order to improve overall efficiency and service. How many of us realise that customer satisfaction in the local superstore could depend upon the way workers pick oranges in Spain?

Read the case study, and then go through the assessment guidelines carefully before you start work.

The Fruits of Training

Increasing numbers of companies are finding that a more European outlook can help their business. Asda has recently run an EU-funded training project, which has given some interesting insights into the totality of customer service.

In a fruit store in Valencia, groups of workers may soon be sitting down to watch a video of shoppers in a Merseyside Asda supermarket. They will observe with interest how 'picky' British shoppers are, rejecting fruit that is bruised or discoloured. On the Continent, people are apparently more interested in the taste than the appearance of their food, and the strange behaviour of the British is something which Asda is very keen to get over to its suppliers.

Asda applied for funding from the programme after it had already conceived a plan for improving the quality of its products by going back to the source. As Margaret McClelland, the company's training schemes manager, puts it: 'We are almost literally going back to our roots.

In a sense, it's a simple version of TQM, looking at quality at every stage of production.'

Asda is one of the pioneers of National Vocational Qualifications (NVQs), and after finding that the training and assessment linked to the scheme improved productivity, quality, communications and loyalty within the stores, Asda wanted to spread the benefits of the system further down the line to its suppliers.

Its ideals were precisely in line with the aims of the European Union's Force programme, which has funded 155 projects, 22 of them led by UK organisations. These aims include disseminating good training practices across national borders, and between large and small companies, involving the social partners (Asda is unionised), encouraging design and implementation of qualifications to meet labour market needs and focusing on people for whom access to training is hard, such as those working in rural areas.

It could almost have been written for Asda and the two suppliers it invited to work on the project: Teresa Hermanos, the Spanish company which picks and distributes the oranges for Asda stores, and Pomanjou, a French company which does the same for apples.

Growing the trees

Emilio Teresa, son of the man who founded the Spanish firm, believes that his firm, along with others in the sector, needs to improve quality, using more training and better technology. He leapt at the chance to use the project to re-examine quality through every stage of production, from growing the trees in the first place to the method of distribution.

At the growing stage, the project may enable the company to draw from the experience of Pomanjou in grafting new varieties onto existing trees. It is also interested in learning new methods of protecting the trees so the fruits do not bang into each other when the wind blows.

When it comes to picking fruit, although it is basically still a matter of people and ladders, they don't – or shouldn't – just yank oranges and apples off their stalks and throw them into a box. There are correct ways of cutting the stalk, and right and wrong methods of packing.

Through the project, the firm intends to introduce new methods of picking and handling, and to train pickers and packers on the job, using an NVQ-type approach.

This is a big project, since the company has four packhouses of its own, with up to 500 pickers and 500 packers in each who work both in the company's own fields and in the orchards of subcontracted growers. 'At the moment, pickers in some cases stand on ladders and then throw the fruit into boxes, although not from a great height, and there are methods we can introduce to improve on this, such as bags to tie to people's chests where they can put the fruit and then undo the bottom of the bag to let the fruit out gently into the box.'

Once picked, the fruit is packed and then shipped to Thames Fruit, the firm's Kent depot, where it is checked for quality and redis-tributed to the stores. Teresa wants to cut out this stage of quality inspection and redistribution in Kent, by training people at the Spanish packhouse to get quality right first time, so fruit could be driven straight to its destination, arriving two days fresher and saving Asda and Teresa Hermanos 15% of their costs.

Distribution chain

This also means training the Spanish truck drivers to understand their place in the distribution chain more clearly, and to know where to go and how to get there, details of store opening times, and so forth.

'The benefits to employees will be in understanding the whole business; and if the training works, we will have a product which is grown properly, picked properly, packed properly, exported properly and transported properly,' he says. 'The British shopper will have a product that is two days younger.'

Pomanjou is intending to concentrate on training packers, learning from the example of NVQs. It has plans to equip all supervisors in the packhouse with books outlining the standards expected in each task. The supervisor will then record when people reach these standards.

The problem for all three countries involved in the project, is translating the work-based training and assessment method into nationally recognised qualifications. Spanish qualifications in the sector exist but Teresa does not believe there is one compatible with NVQs. Similarly in France, national qualifications can only be obtained through conventional examinations.

Annick Guyet, the project co-ordinator at Pomanjou, explains that to enable a work-based system to gain national recognition would be an immensely convoluted business, as it is in Britain, involving organisations representing the sector nationally and the government. Without this, she is concerned that the employees themselves will see little point in the exercise.

McClelland found that NVQs 'emphasise

how important people are and they can see their contribution more clearly and look more closely at what they do themselves'. Figures to prove the worth of NVQs are hard to establish, she says. But there has been an increase in productivity in the last 12 months in stores where they have been piloted. 'We think the general effect of NVQs and other things we are doing is that they have a knock-on effect among the people not taking part.'

NVQs have been successfully implemented at the Hunt's Cross store in Merseyside. According to the Personnel and Training Manager, the great attraction of NVQs is the magic words 'City and Guilds' attached to the retail certificate. 'I have women saying to me: "Oh, City and Guilds. My son has that. Do you really mean I could have that too?" ' she says.

Another advantage of the pilot appears to have been in the increase in company loyalty among those employees undertaking NVQs. Long says that not one of the people who achieved certificates in the last two years has left.

Meanwhile, as well as providing half the funding to develop supplier training, the Force project is helping Asda to build on its NVQ work, introducing levels 3 and 4 of the retail certificate in some stores and business administration 1 and 2 in others.

There is also some pilot work for the Management Charter Initiative going on and McClelland herself, already a good French speaker, expects to learn Spanish to help her in the project.

Where Asda or its suppliers go in terms of developing qualifications after the end of the Force project is unclear. But what is certain is that all three partners feel they are benefiting from it.

This article is reproduced with the permission of *P M Plus*, the magazine of the Institute of Personnel Management.

Guidelines and requirements for Assessment One

You will probably need to read the Asda case study a couple of times to make sure you have grasped the main ideas, and you may wish to raise some points with your tutor in order to clarify your understanding.

If you are college based, the initial activity revolves around group work, and you should form yourselves into discussion groups of four or five people in order to consider the implications of your main task in this section. If you are home based, you may wish to raise questions with your tutor before embarking on the task.

Task

Produce a paper to be presented at a regional forum being organised by the local Chamber of Commerce for retail managers and training specialists. Your paper should draw on Asda's experience and identify a range of influences that have contributed to the project – ie forces and agents of change.

Any discussions you have could be very useful in bringing out and clarifying ideas, and you should make notes of these ideas as you go along. At the end of the discussion period (approximately one hour if you are in college) you will be expected to work on *your own paper*.

Some general themes to help with your planning and/or discussion are listed below and these will also give you some guidelines on how to structure your written submission. Your tutors may be able to contribute further ideas or help you with general background information on some aspects.

Planning/Discussion themes

- The general theme of the paper
- The overall aim of the Asda project
- Specific objectives of the project
- Change and the European influence
- Costs, funding and government influence on change
- What was the business plan?
- What did the participants hope to achieve? What were their roles? What specific job areas were involved? Were there likely to be any job losses?
- What function do recognised qualifications have? What are NVQs?
- What problems are there with the compatibility of qualifications?
- Was the project successful? Why? How?
- Identify as many different groups of people involved in the project as you can, who you think were being affected by 'change'. Explain how.
- What are the implications for other companies, if any?

Notes

What is a 'paper'?

- A formal document designed to present a structured series of ideas/arguments relevant to a particular theme. A conclusion is often, but not always, required.
- It is often used as the basis for an oral presentation, but must *not* be written as a verbatim speech – that is, not in direct speech.
- The structure should be logical, and must be appropriate to the audience: Who are they? What is their background? What are they interested in?
- The paper needs a thematic *title* which immediately conveys the overall purpose of giving the information.
- When writing a paper, you must be clear of its aim. What do you want to achieve? (In this case the aim is to convince experienced business people that their companies can benefit from a co-ordinated programme of review/evaluation of procedures, and formally structured training schemes – it is worth the investment.)
- The *style of writing* is important: it should be formal, abstract (like a report), not personalised.

*Possible structure for
Assessment One: Asda paper*
(you may use the headings indicated)

Heading: Paper produced for Plymouth Chamber of Commerce

Forum on ....*(theme title)* ....

Venue: ....

Quality for the customer
The importance of total customer service and TQM in the retail industry, and the need to constantly review/evaluate processes and procedures.

The Asda Project
Principles; aims – looking at the whole operation associated with the delivery of fruit to the customers. (Don't emphasise money-saving aspects at this stage.)

Change – a dirty word!
Problems associated with changing people's attitudes and working practices – general theory.

Training and qualifications
The use of co-ordinated training programmes leading to formal, recognised qualifications to motivate for change. Problems of compatibility across Europe? Use the Asda case study for specific examples.

The benefits
The benefits for any company in such a programme of review, evaluation and training – efficiency, quality, productivity, customer satisfaction, costs, market share, etc.

Unit 3

**Resisting progress or
protecting working
conditions?**

Reading 1 If we think about an office environment and consider how dramatic
the changes caused by the introduction of modern technology
might be, it is easy to identify general concerns which influence
people's reactions.

The most basic concern is usually *economic*. Is the introduction
of the new equipment going to result in job losses, cuts in hours, or
the closing of complete sections/departments? Nobody wants to be
made redundant, or have their economic stability threatened, and
unless employees can be convinced that they will not 'lose out',
there is likely to be opposition, or at least non-co-operation.

Another important consideration revolves around each individual's perceived social position. Even basic office re-organisation
(changing desks around) can be seen as a threat to established social
relationships:

'I've always worked well with Shirley.'
'I don't want to work with him.'
'Who am I going to have to sit next to?'
'I know how he thinks.'
'We've got this job well organised.'

The problem of having to form new working relationships, or
even join a new group can be upsetting and quite daunting to many
people.

If a functional area of an organisation is being completely
restructured, with consequent transfers, promotions, new supervisors or managers, the problems are magnified.

Another area of concern is often the individual's *personal fears*.
Will they have to learn a new skill? Do they have the ability to learn
a new skill? Will they be able to cope with the different work? What
will this do to their health? The range of personal fears is enormous, and even though they are sometimes founded on lack of
understanding, they are very real, and affect people's response to
change.

The results of all these fears and concerns can, of course, affect
the running of the organisation, and might be manifested in a number of ways (Figure 5).

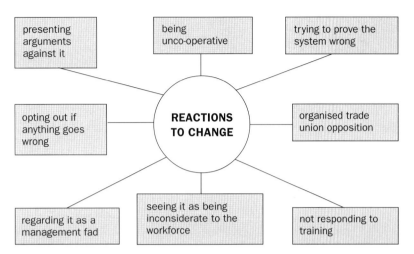

Figure 5 Reactions to change in an organisation

As you can see, the managers and the supervisors could have a difficult task on their hands in some organisations, and it is the recognition of this that is likely to lead to a greater appreciation of the *human relations* aspects of introducing change. If consideration is shown for *people*, then those people are more likely to show a willingness to listen and, hopefully, to co-operate.

Reading 2   Much research has been conducted on change and its effects, and it is clear that there is a tendency among employees to resist anything that affects their current working conditions/practices – even though it is likely that they would benefit from improvements. Once change has been introduced, however, it is quite common for employees to turn around and say that they prefer the new arrangements to the old! However, there is often an 'in-between' time when initial opposition, sometimes accompanied by industrial action, makes life very difficult for supervisors, managers and policy makers. We can identify some general reasons for resistance to change:

- Important and permanent decisions about an employee's working life are made by people who have little or no contact with him or her in normal circumstances.

- The employee may lose the job or be transferred to a lower-paid job.

- The skill and experience the employee has acquired over the years may suddenly become redundant in the context of new job requirements.

- The employee's status in the firm may be lower.

- Cohesive social groups may be broken up with a consequent disruption in established relationships, roles and norms.

- New relationships must be established, new 'rules' learned.

- Patterns of working that people are used to represent security; anything new often creates insecurity.

- Personal life may be affected by new working times or a transfer to a new area.

Each individual will, of course, demonstrate a different attitude to change – some will welcome it and the associated excitement and break from routine; others dislike any change in their working or personal lives. Obviously, the reactions will depend on the type and extent of change, and on the way it is introduced. (Look again at Figure 5 to remind yourself how such concerns can manifest themselves.)

Unit 4

**Managing and
implementing change**

Reading 1 **Overcoming resistance to change**

If we know what causes resistance to change, how do we overcome it? There are many ideas put forward by a variety of managers, management theorists and management consultants. Some of these are summarised in the following notes.

(a) *Pilot schemes:* where changes are introduced in limited areas for a trial period. After, say, six months, the 'experiment' is reviewed and the general pattern is that at this stage a degree of reverse-opposition is identified – ie workers do not want to return to the old ways of working.

(b)

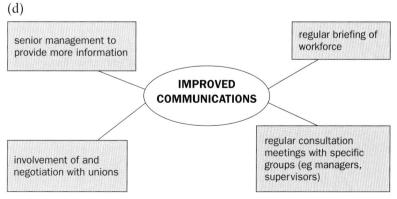

Figure 6 Offering financial incentives as a means of overcoming resistance to change in an organisation

guaranteed maintenance of earnings levels

no compulsory redundancies

FINANCIAL INCENTIVES

any reduction in workforce by natural wastage

finance made available for training/re-training schemes

(c) *Small-scale changes:* rather than wait until things reach a crisis point, and large-scale changes are forced upon a workforce, management teams should try to engender an atmosphere of continuous change, making minor adjustments and amendments to work practices on a regular basis as part of a review, efficiency and quality control policy. Change then becomes normal and acceptable.

(d)

senior management to provide more information

regular briefing of workforce

IMPROVED COMMUNICATIONS

Figure 7 Improving communications as a means of overcoming resistance to change in an organisation

involvement of and negotiation with unions

regular consultation meetings with specific groups (eg managers, supervisors)

(e) *Management/supervisory pressure:* this can only be successful if a manager has built up a very good working relationship with staff and a fund of goodwill. As it relies on an authoritarian concept, it should be regarded as a short-term solution.

(f)

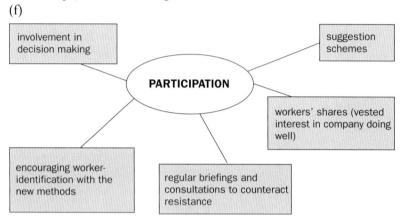

Figure 8 Encouraging worker participation as a means of overcoming resistance to change in an organisation

Reading 2 Managing change

The survival of any company will depend upon the management's ability to identify the need for change, exploit opportunities, and persuade the workforce to adjust their work practices accordingly. Whether the change is minor or major, it is management's responsibility to ensure a thorough understanding of the pressures for change and the benefits for the whole organisation – it is no good simply improving employees' performance, if the increased productivity results in a stockpile of goods that cannot be sold. The emphasis must be on effective *worthwhile* improvement, which enables the company – and the employees – to reap the rewards of their success.

In the context of management, there are many criticisms that can be made of traditional, hide-bound attitudes based on an authoritarian approach and an unwillingness to 'rock the boat'. Fortunately, managerial attitudes have changed dramatically in recent years, and the effective manager is aware that his/her influence on certain crucial areas can have a dramatic effect on employee attitudes and reactions. Here are some things a forward-looking manager will aim to do:

■ Implement an effective recruitment and selection policy.

■ Demonstrate required standards of behaviour by personal example.

- Avoid political manoeuvring which could be seen as being based on self-interest.

- Remove any 'system of rights' which gives unfair perks or unearned financial gain to any individual.

- Stamp out favouritism.

- Introduce new technology to keep abreast of change.

- Implement appropriate policies to counteract sexual harassment and unfair treatment.

- Create an atmosphere of mutual trust.

- Establish an effective appraisal scheme and career development programme.

- Consult regularly with all employee groups.

Reading 3 A synopsis of the principles associated with introducing and implementing change is not difficult to produce, as the statements that can be made and the conclusions that can be drawn stem from common sense.

Change is now an ever-present part of everyday life, and we can expect the pace to increase – particularly in the workplace where the main responsibility will fall on management and supervisory staff for introducing and managing the process. This will be an ongoing commitment requiring constant planning and review. Although change can be thrust upon an organisation without warning (unplanned), it is more likely that an effective management team will anticipate the needs and adopt a strategy of careful preparation, informed introduction and planned implementation.

Influences for change are numerous and can come from almost any direction: economic (eg shortages of resources); technological (eg changes in processes, procedures, materials); the market (eg competition, consumer 'whim'); sociological (eg ecological trends, consumer buying patterns, industrial relations).

Wherever the pressure comes from, individuals will react to change in many different ways. Some will welcome it, but the majority are likely to manifest responses including disbelief, shock, antagonism, depression or fear. Feelings of insecurity or uncertainty will be reinforced by concerns about learning new skills, losing income, having to change job or even possible redundancy. It's not surprising that managers and supervisors feel under pressure when they know that change is imminent, but things can go more smoothly if a coherent plan is established. Some standard approaches will help implementers to maximise the advantages and minimise the disadvantages:

1   Give all employees who are likely to be affected the maximum warning that changes are coming, thus giving them time to get used to the idea.

2   Provide a clear explanation of the reasons for change, avoiding damaging rumours and letting people know exactly where they stand.

3   Consider the effects of change on individuals – their personal fears, concerns and aspirations. Acknowledge the fact that individual counselling might be necessary, and facilitate this.

4   Involve individual employees, product teams, established sections or any other groups in the planning process. This will encourage commitment and a two-way communication, and can often result in useful suggestions being put forward to help the process.

5   Emphasise and publicise the benefits of the change, explaining how things like job-enrichment, increased responsibility, improved prospects and conditions can benefit the individual. It might even be prudent to include some financial incentives.

6   Don't try to change everything at once – introduce changes gradually, and implement a phased strategy if this is possible.

7   Encourage, and provide the financial resources for, appropriate training. Nobody can be expected to adapt to new skills, new equipment, new procedures, etc without some feelings of apprehension or insecurity, and effective training can counteract this, ensuring a smooth transition.

8   Try to minimise changes in current work patterns, effective work teams and individual preferences. Obviously there will have to be some changes, but change for the sake of change is likely to cause dissatisfaction and conflict.

9   Communication is all-important – monitor progress, facilitate regular feedback, and regularly inform all parts of the workforce on how things are going.

10 Conduct 'follow-up' activities – talk to people, see how they are coping, give support where necessary.

The following reference table might help you remember the basic strategies for implementing change:

Inform	Keep staff fully informed of what is going on, even at the planning stage.
Discuss	Find out what the staff think, what their fears are and what their needs/expectations are.
Consult	The staff might have some good ideas which can be used, based on practical experience, or some sound objections which could save you time/money.
Brief	Give as much instruction/information as possible to help staff adjust to new systems.
Train	Provide effective training and allow time for training.
Counsel	Allow for counselling and further training as the system is implemented, to iron out the wrinkles – things will go wrong!

Assessment Two

Units 3 and 4 deal with the practical implications of change from a human relations and management point of view, and this case study of a Civil Service department in the West Midlands shows how a planned approach, positive leadership and effective teamwork can transform the operation of what is often regarded by the customers as a bureaucratic nightmare. You will find references to the concept of total quality management (TQM), and there is an additional reading on this topic on page 29. The West Midlands approach should give you a clear insight into how it can work. Quality control and TQM are important concepts, and a unit is devoted to them in Section Four.

Task and guidelines

You will certainly need to read through the case study a couple of times to get the 'flavour' of what has happened in this government department. This assessment requires you to write a report reviewing the implementation of change and the effects on various aspects of this organisation. As a Communications Officer with the West Midlands authority you have been approached by your opposite number in the East Midlands authority for some information on how the 'experiment' has gone. You discuss the situation with your senior officer and eventually receive authorisation from the Regional Director to draft a report covering the aspects of the scheme as set out below. He requests that the report is submitted to him so that he can 'clear' it before it is sent to your colleague in the East Midlands authority.

You should adopt a *short formal report format* (see Figure 9) and include information on the following points:

■ The situation in the West Midlands authority before the change

■ Why there was a need for change

■ What example(s) influenced the change

■ What resistance to change was identified/overcome

- The 'Business Plan' – ie aims; how the changes were implemented (eg workshops, training schemes, consultation, teamwork, etc); the strategy

- The result of the change (on the organisations, for managers/ supervisors, physical changes, attitude changes, technical changes, for customers, efficiency, etc)

- The future

- Conclusions (successful or unsuccessful?)

Note: You should agree an outline structure for your report with your tutors (ie the heading and subheading sequence) *before* you start to write up detailed information. Some ideas on classification of information and overall content are given on page 30.

For the attention of ....

Full and explanatory title

1 TERMS OF REFERENCE ('Introduction' can be used)
This should indicate the scope of the report, the background to the situation, any specific source material, and why the report is being submitted.

2 PROCEDURE
Explain accurately and concisely how the research was conducted – how the information was collected, who was interviewed, etc.

3 FINDINGS   **Notes:**
  (a) Subheading   *These should be presented schematically. The number*
      i)   *of main sections, the number of subsections, and the*
      ii)   *extent of the individual comments will depend on the*
      iii)   *information you have available and the requirements*
  (b) Subheading   *of the recipient.* **Do not use note form.** *The sequence of*
      i)   *subheadings should be logical and, as far as possible,*
      ii)   *in rank order.*
      iii)
  (c) Subheading
      i)
      ii)
      iii)

4 CONCLUSIONS
These can be presented as a narrative paragraph, or a number of points. In the latter case, accurate cross-referencing with main findings is desirable. A continuation of the schematic presentation can be used if appropriate.

5 RECOMMENDATIONS
See comments on 'Conclusions' Recommendations should not be included unless specifically asked for.

                    Signature: ....
                    Designation: ....
                    Date: ....

Figure 9 General layout for a short formal report

Reading 4   Total quality management (TQM)

Any effective manager will be aware of the need for planned strategies for implementing change, but any manager who has responsibility for monitoring and controlling work activities will also be aware that certain management strategies in this area can themselves be catalysts for change.

Total quality management (TQM) is the name given to the process and management of change in pursuit of quality. All aspects of the organisation are involved, from the mission through the overall culture to the day-to-day working practices – all continuously working towards improvement.

The essential philosophy behind TQM is that anything can be improved, but the process can be complex and demanding and must be integrated with traditional strategies for implementing change. Total quality will normally stem from the need to satisfy customers, so contact and consultation with them is crucial. A 'customer' can be external, in the traditional sense, or internal – ie anyone who depends on another's 'products' in order to fulfil his or her own role. There will be many obstacles to overcome and many problems to be solved if people are to be *enabled* to do their best: there might be a need for additional investment in equipment, facilities or training; a *management by objectives* approach might be desirable so that everyone knows what is expected of them and what progress is being made; participative management will need to be encouraged so that people will feel involved and will work together in pursuit of improvement; review and evaluation procedures will become a normal part of life and will be welcomed as an aid to monitoring, control and improvement.

As all these developments are accepted, an overall TQM culture will be established which will create a climate in which people are not automatically satisfied with current performance; in which there is an overt commitment to the needs, interests, requirements and expectations of customers; in which management attitudes and approaches clearly promote a commitment to quality; and in which on-going training programmes ensure that staff are given every opportunity to improve their personal skills and performance.

With TQM embedded in its culture, the organisation will have a competitive advantage because customers will seek out a company that offers quality products or services. Employees themselves will find that work becomes more interesting because they are involved in decision making and have responsibility for getting things done (job enrichment). There will be more job satisfaction because tasks will be completed more effectively and efficiently, and possibly more job security, because an efficient organisation is invariably more profitable when the costs of poor quality are overcome.

Some ideas for the West Midlands Employment Service report

These notes are designed to guide you towards a logical and coherent structure for the report. You should plan your heading sequence and overall classification of information independently, and can add any further ideas of your own.

1   Pay attention to Figure 9.

2   Ensure that the 'Terms of reference' and 'Procedure' sections are appropriately written.

3   It would be useful to start the main body of the report with a summary of the situation as it was, identifying the need for change and some of the problems associated with it. You can refer to examples that influenced change, and when commenting on any resistance shown by the workforce, introduce aspects of theory that you have studied in this unit.

4   There will need to be an explanation of the aims of the changes introduced, and a full description of strategies used for implementation.

5   Once you move on to the results of the re-organisation, it is important to identify the effects not only on the organisation, but also on the staff and the customers. Some reference to environmental changes could also be helpful.

6   From the recipient's point of view, it would be useful to know how you see the future.

7   A short general conclusion will be appropriate.

TQM in the public sector

When total quality management gained prominence in Britain, it tended to be associated with the manufacturing sector. More recently it has been gaining ground in the public sector, and Jane Pickard describes how it is applied in a Civil Service department: 'Our basic recruitment demand was five O-levels, but we sometimes treated them like automatons: everything was laid down and you could almost have got a robot to do what they did.'

'They' are staff at Jobcentres and unemployment benefit offices in the West Midlands. Describing their plight is the Employment Service's regional director, Martin Raff. Anyone who worked with him five or ten years ago – he was briefly in charge of personnel for the MSC – would be astonished to hear him talk now. Raff, who had a reputation for being something of a tyrant, has been converted to total quality management. In his own words, he has changed from being 'a very demanding and prescriptive leader to being much more a team player and team leader. People say now they are more relaxed and feel happier in the team, and there is more openness and honesty. They are able to speak frankly about their difficulties.'

On a more scientific level, the region has moved from the bottom of the league table on performance indicators to near the middle. Raff's next ambition is to rank first on the most important of these: the numbers of unemployed placed in jobs – which he believes they might achieve by the end of the year.

The turning point for him was a visit to the Nissan factory in Northumberland over three years ago. He went to look at communications systems and found the whole approach to management 'quite mind-boggling'. He saw similarities between the Nissan production teams and Employment Service teams: 'The difference between what they were getting out of their people and what we were getting out of ours was quite dramatic.'

Since then his region has been pioneering total quality management in the service, drawing directly from the principles developed by Dr W. Edwards Deming, one of the American pioneers of the quality movement. The region is now regarded by many as one of the most advanced examples of such an approach in the British public sector.

One of the things that interested Raff about the Nissan plant was the use of statistical process control, a technique developed by statistician Walter Shewart in the 1920s and perfected by Deming and fellow professional Joseph Juran. It aims to maintain quality during a process, cutting down on end-of-line inspection. 'To my knowledge this had never been used in a clerical process, and I thought we could try it out.'

He appointed Julie Beedon, a regional office manager with a maths and statistics degree, as quality co-ordinator and, after running trials in two offices, they set up a quality committee of senior managers to transform the region's culture, staff attitudes and performance. They were advised by Peter Worthington and his colleagues from the Prism consultancy.

The committee introduced a training programme combining background and Deming's theories with an introduction to the techniques of statistical process control. Workshops started with the senior management team, area managers and regional office section heads, then covered managers of the 110 Jobcentres and unemployment benefit offices, followed by a launch day for each office, which the entire staff attended. The day included basic training in 'variation' theory, using simple experiments to demonstrate the degree to which management systems, rather than individual performance, led to varied quality. Each office manager then planned four days of training for small groups of staff, which has been gradually extended so everyone is now covered.

However, the training was not carried out in isolation. Other changes which were started immediately before quality management surfaced, are now bound up in what has become a major culture change in the region. One of these was the idea of turning old-fashioned Civil Service managers into 'active leaders', trying to enthuse instead of dictate.

Another visible demonstration of Raff's determination to change attitudes has been a move to an 'open-plan' format throughout the region, both in terms of dismantling counters between staff and customers – a national policy anyway – and getting managers out of their offices. Raff himself now works in a huge open-plan area.

However, he has resisted imposing this change on anyone. Getting rid of counters in offices has been fiercely resisted by unions nationally. But in the West Midlands all but three counters have gone, despite that fact that staff were able to vote on it, and only three out of 110 managers (not the same three) have refused to leave their offices.

By themselves, Raff says, the moves to open plan, active leadership, and a number of other measures such as customer-focus training, worked only in pockets. He is convinced that what really triggered the change was the way the quality philosophy brought all their efforts into focus as part of a greater whole, and the methodology it provided to measure quality and make a continuous series of improvements.

Staff echo this. At a combined Jobcentre and benefit office in Cheylesmore, Coventry, managers discussed the combination of changed attitudes and new techniques. One said: 'There is more opportunity for operators to influence improvements and people are actively interested in their own job. They no longer hand the problem-solving automatically to managers. The manager's role has become one of facilitating these kinds of improvements.'

Some of the changes are physical and cultural: the office is open plan, it has been redecorated in shades of pink, managers sit out 'on the section' with staff, and relationships between staff and customers and among staff themselves appear to be more respectful.

Other changes are technical: the 85 staff have formed quality teams looking in painstaking detail at ways they could improve the rate of placing unemployed people into jobs, the speed with which a benefit claim is processed onto the computer, and similar issues.

On these issues and on other projects, the team have made great strides. However, the team that achieved and exceeded the national objective of getting 90% of new claimants' details onto the computer within six days from a starting point of 40%, has now turned its atten-

tion to something else. What they could have done, in the spirit of continuous improvement, was to reduce the target deadline to, say, three days.

This illustrates one of the problems with targets which Deming himself has pinpointed. He warns against them on the grounds that they induce either complacency or over-anxiety or defeatism. But the region has to work to nationally-set performance indicators.

Deming has also criticised bonuses tied to individual performance on the grounds that it is the management system that affects performance rather than the individual.

This raises another problem for the West Midlands region. Like it or not – and the Civil Service unions, among others, do not – performance-related pay (PRP) will be introduced from on high as a result of government policy.

Raff and Beedon say the region can capitalise in its own way on PRP, linking it to personal goals rather than office targets. But Raff adds, 'You have to unpack Deming a bit. Some consultants treat it as a religion you cannot diverge from, but we don't take that attitude.'

Malcolm Owens, regional human resources manager, points out that the decentralisation of personnel two years ago into branch offices, working alongside the office manager, has not only helped in the quality programme but, together with TQM, has contributed to the new culture that will enable PRP to work in an enlightened way.

'Since the managers are working in teams, they will know more about the people they are working with, which should make the appraisal system fairer. The more people work together and get rid of these hierarchical barriers, whatever appraisal system you have should be more effective. It will help to stop people blaming each other, if they really understand what causes the problems in an office.'

In fact, the personnel function is a good illustration of how quality management in the public sector not only has to cope with the conflicts of working within a national, non-TQM system, but can help sort out the red tape which itself threatens to strangle the TQM.

The main role of personnel at Owens' level is to interpret national regulations in local offices. In the past this was done by 'handing down edicts on tablets of stone'. Now, working in partnership with line management, personnel is using graphic design to present the regulations in a comprehensible way, and working through dozens of forms to clarify their layout and discard requests for needless information.

'We have had working groups tracing the route of a form and spotting where errors occur and why. Once you have gone through that process it is surprising how many boxes people normally have to fill in which can be scrapped,' says Owens.

The question remains: Is it impossible to take a true quality approach in the public sector while still being tangled up with Civil Service red tape and subservient to national dictate?

The two main Civil Service unions, which back the West Midlands scheme, say it is. They want a national evaluation and believe there is an inherent conflict between quality and performance pay.

Beedon says it isn't. In fact, she says the Employment Service and Employment Department have been extremely supportive. However, the Employment Service refuses to adopt the West Midlands approach as a national policy, since it believes in decentralised management.

This article is reproduced with the permission of *P M Plus*, the magazine of the Institute of Personnel Management.

Groups and group behaviour

Unit 5

Introduction and summary of principles

The influence of groups on our lives is not always fully appreciated, as most of us like to think of ourselves as individuals. However, it is a fact that we are all subject to group influence, and our attitudes, prejudices and whole outlook on life have been created through our experiences as members of groups.

Let's start with the basics, and think about how we think. How are our attitudes formed? Figure 10 gives an indication of some major influences on all of us.

SOCIALISATION

The way our parents/teachers/ schools have influenced our thinking by direct teaching or by simply involving us in activities and discussions.

EXPERIENCE

Everything that happens to us affects our view of the world, and attitudes can be formed very quickly if we are subjected to an experience that affects the running of our lives.

ATTITUDES

GROUPS

Friends and colleagues bring in new ideas as we get older, and we often adapt to and adopt the prevalent attitudes of the social or work group to which we wish to belong. These might, of course, conflict with earlier attitudes and lead to 'misunderstandings' with parents!

Figure 10 Some influences on personal attitudes

In any of these situations, the right conditions have been presented to form or change our attitudes, and very often a change of attitudes is simply the formation of a new one in place of an old one.

This simplistic explanation might make it sound as if it is easy to persuade someone to change their outlook, but nothing could be further from the truth. The reason for this is that our attitudes are usually influenced and reinforced by people for whom we have respect, love or admiration, and by experiences which have directly affected the way in which we run our lives. Our attitudes and actions often bring us 'rewards', such as social approval, acceptance by a group, admiration, respect, congratulations, even promotion.

Thus we can see that groups are important to us. At work you are likely to be a member of a formal group, which has been established by management to perform a particular task or fulfil a particular role in the working of the organisation. This might be a department, or a section, or a small subgroup of specialists. As well as this formal grouping, you can probably identify a number of people with whom you like to spend your break-times or lunch-times, and who can loosely be described as a group of friends. These informal groups are equally important to you as an individual, and can have a positive function in the life of the organisation, ensuring cross-fertilisation of ideas, speedy communication and rapid feedback.

Whatever the group, most members have joined it voluntarily, and it stands to reason that each individual is deriving benefit from membership. Hopefully, the group is benefiting from the contribution made by each individual, and the organisation is benefiting from having a well-integrated workforce. It's pretty obvious that the interaction between the individual and the various groups to which he or she belongs is of great importance.

Groups are a fact of life, but why do people join them? It's unlikely that any of us have sat down and thoroughly analysed our reasons for working in the Accounts Section, or joining the darts team, or representing our colleagues on the Social Committee, but consider some of the ideas presented in Figure 11.

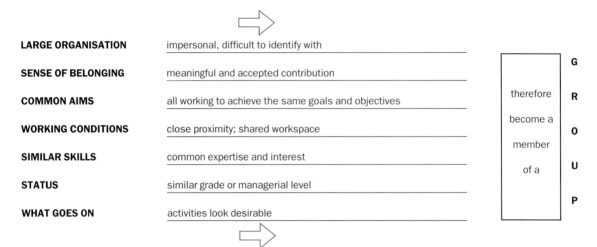

LARGE ORGANISATION	impersonal, difficult to identify with		G
SENSE OF BELONGING	meaningful and accepted contribution		R
COMMON AIMS	all working to achieve the same goals and objectives	therefore	
WORKING CONDITIONS	close proximity; shared workspace	become a	O
SIMILAR SKILLS	common expertise and interest	member	
STATUS	similar grade or managerial level	of a	U
WHAT GOES ON	activities look desirable		P

Figure 11 Some reasons for becoming a member of a group

To express things in a slightly different way, individuals join groups for various reasons – for example:

- to improve their effectiveness in a task
- for security
- to facilitate learning through social comparison
- to exert greater influence over their environment
- because they believe that group membership will be useful to them in the achievement of some goal in the future.

Activity 3

As stated at the beginning of this unit, most people prefer to think of themselves as individuals rather than as members of a group or organisation. However, as you will have realised from the preceding comments, it is virtually impossible for anyone to exist as a total isolationist and, in any case, being a member of a group does not mean that you are obliged to forfeit your individualism or become a clone.

Think carefully about this very general definition of a group:

A recognisable collection of people, organised formally or informally, whose interrelationships are based on a range of identifiable characteristics.
Is such a definition accurate? Does it have any drawbacks?

Task   Produce your own definition of a group (maximum 50 words), bearing in mind the ideas and explanations given here and your own knowledge of how groups affect your life.

The 'identifiable characteristics' mentioned in the definition on page 36 are outlined in Figure 12. Consider the instructions and questions posed in the 'Tasks' column, and produce written commentaries based on your own experiences at work, at college or in social groups. You should aim to include at least one work-based and one social group. In your commentaries you should give a balanced picture by discussing a range of formal and informal groups.

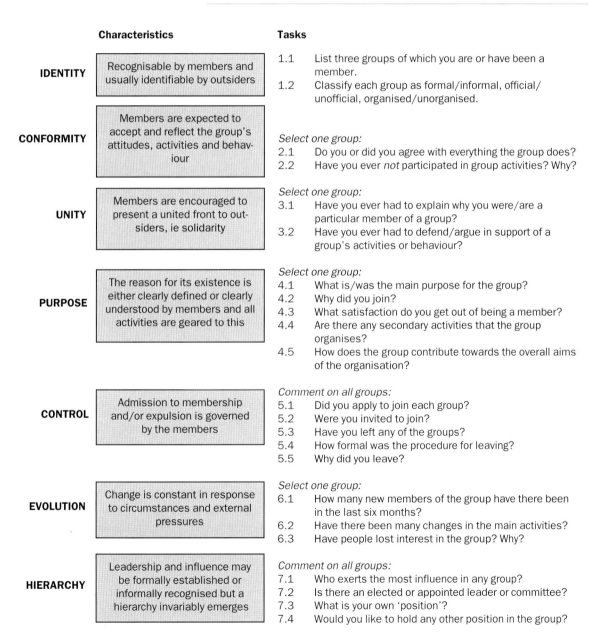

Characteristics	Tasks
IDENTITY — Recognisable by members and usually identifiable by outsiders	1.1 List three groups of which you are or have been a member. 1.2 Classify each group as formal/informal, official/unofficial, organised/unorganised.
CONFORMITY — Members are expected to accept and reflect the group's attitudes, activities and behaviour	*Select one group:* 2.1 Do you or did you agree with everything the group does? 2.2 Have you ever *not* participated in group activities? Why?
UNITY — Members are encouraged to present a united front to outsiders, ie solidarity	*Select one group:* 3.1 Have you ever had to explain why you were/are a particular member of a group? 3.2 Have you ever had to defend/argue in support of a group's activities or behaviour?
PURPOSE — The reason for its existence is either clearly defined or clearly understood by members and all activities are geared to this	*Select one group:* 4.1 What is/was the main purpose for the group? 4.2 Why did you join? 4.3 What satisfaction do you get out of being a member? 4.4 Are there any secondary activities that the group organises? 4.5 How does the group contribute towards the overall aims of the organisation?
CONTROL — Admission to membership and/or expulsion is governed by the members	*Comment on all groups:* 5.1 Did you apply to join each group? 5.2 Were you invited to join? 5.3 Have you left any of the groups? 5.4 How formal was the procedure for leaving? 5.5 Why did you leave?
EVOLUTION — Change is constant in response to circumstances and external pressures	*Select one group:* 6.1 How many new members of the group have there been in the last six months? 6.2 Have there been many changes in the main activities? 6.3 Have people lost interest in the group? Why?
HIERARCHY — Leadership and influence may be formally established or informally recognised but a hierarchy invariably emerges	*Comment on all groups:* 7.1 Who exerts the most influence in any group? 7.2 Is there an elected or appointed leader or committee? 7.3 What is your own 'position'? 7.4 Would you like to hold any other position in the group?

Figure 12 Identifiable characteristics of a group

How groups function

In attempting the previous activity you will probably have touched on some of the points dealt with in the summary that follows, and this should help you relate the theory to your own experience.

It is a fact that large groups tend to split themselves up into smaller groups in which communication and interaction between individuals is easier. The smaller group allows for the quieter and rather shy person to be drawn into activities or discussions, and for all members to make a useful contribution. But does this mean that a large group is ineffective? Obviously it depends on the situation, because in some circumstances 'many hands make light work', and in others 'too many cooks spoil the broth'.

In the work situation, it is likely that any group will be subject to certain requirements such as co-ordination, common aims, agreed strategies, etc. Studies have shown that in such circumstances it appears that the larger the group, the greater the degree of co-ordination and control needed, and this can lead to individual dis-satisfaction, an increase in absenteeism and labour turnover, low motivation levels, and greater frequency of error. It is the unenviable task of management to identify optimum group size and help create an efficient working environment.

Within any group, the individuals, their interests and characteristics will help determine its effectiveness. If attitudes, ideas and motivations are similar, stability is relatively easy to maintain; if there is a wide variety of beliefs and approaches, there will be disagreements and possibly conflict, needing a high degree of co-ordination and organisation to create a positive working environment. The formation of group 'norms' will be recognised by all members and they may be informally 'understood' or written down in formal regulations governing activities and behaviour. It is the wish to be accepted which helps to hold the group together, and even the most informal of group requirements is likely to be adhered to because most people need to feel a sense of belonging and do not wish to be seen as being different. The pressure to conform is very strong. Each individual decides the extent to which he or she needs to adapt to fit in with group norms, and, therefore, we all change a little when we join a group. We are influenced by others, and in turn influence others.

Group decision making

One of the most important (and indefinable) processes in business is that of decision making. A decision can be made by an individual or a group, but that made by a group is normally more important and binding than that made by an individual. If *you* make a decision to do something, it is quite easy to change your mind if nobody else is involved. If, however, you're a member of a committee which decides on a course of action, it is not quite so easy to get things changed.

Another aspect of group decision making is that a number of people acting together are more likely to make high-risk decisions than an individual. The spread of responsibility makes people feel that there is 'safety in numbers' and, therefore, they feel confident that they cannot be blamed personally if anything goes wrong. The dangers of group decision making stem from the influence that some individuals can exert on others, and from the pressure to conform.

Bearing in mind some of the comments made in this section, it would be quite easy to accept a sweeping generalisation which claimed that a work group that is of optimum operational size, and in which all the members are happy and satisfied, will be highly productive and efficient. However, we have to be realistic, and accept that it is likely to be a rare occurrence that such a 'perfect' group is created. There will usually be strong characters who pull the group in one direction or another, and influential members who persuade others towards particular courses of action. There are always likely to be some points of disagreement, and this in turn can lead to conflict and dissatisfaction if management does not identify the problems and work towards establishing harmonious working relationships. If a strong leader can be identified, who recognises and supports management/group/section objectives, then half the battle is won, and a thorough and sensitive approach to consultation and appraisal can often prevent minor dissatisfactions and disagreements turning into major conflicts.

Unit 6

Groups – their types and purpose

In the workplace, we can identify three main types of group, but there may well be a variety of subgroups identifiable under each heading.

1 *Executive or command groups (primary groups – formal)*

   ■ consist of managers and their staff

   ■ are involved in planning, organising, motivating, and co-ordinating

   ■ are often specialist in nature

   ■ the group leader (manager) is often the link with other groups

   ■ all groups work towards organisational aims and objectives

   ■ are classified as a formal group.

2 *Committees, project groups, task groups (secondary groups – formal)*

   ■ can be long term (eg an on-going Safety Committee) or short term (formed to perform a specific project)

   ■ long-term groups will often have a structure which does not change when membership changes (eg the Housing Committee of a local authority)

   ■ can be very formal, with elected officers, rules and procedures; or less formal, with a group leader and freedom of operation.

Note: Project or task groups often cut across normal organisational structure, and therefore improve lateral communication, co-operation and co-ordination.

A formal group at work

3   *Informal groups*

- There is a wide variety of these, ranging from casual, ad-hoc meetings to deal with specific work problems, to social groups.

- Some advantages are psychological security (safety in numbers); identity/status; friendship/support; reinforcement of personal attitudes/ideas; informal communication network, source of ideas and solution to problems.

Why does an organisation need groups?

1   *To carry out tasks too complex for an individual* For example, to run a successful racing car team needs people with a range of skills and talents who must work together co-operatively. However, each member of the team has his own duties and responsibilities and the work is distributed amongst the team, according to their individual skills.

2   *To aid effective management and control* A group could have a specific responsibility within the organisation, such as Organisation and Methods (O & M), and would be expected to ensure that this was carried out effectively and efficiently. Such a group would evolve to deal with a specialism demanded by the organisation.

3   *To make decisions and solve problems* The combined knowledge and experience of a number of people should result in better-quality decisions. Many public organisations make extensive use of committees to decide both policy and the priority of objectives. Implementation is then delegated to the full-time employees of the appropriate department.

4   *For arbitration, conciliation and negotiation processes* A carefully constructed group will provide a variety of individuals with a wide spread of values, ideas and beliefs which will give a more objective approach to solving disputes of various kinds. There is also a legal requirement to have a broad spectrum of representatives on bodies such as industrial and administrative tribunals.

5   *To involve workers in decision making* If people are allowed to put forward their own ideas and these are thoroughly discussed, then whether or not they are adopted there will be a stronger commitment to seek a successful outcome than if the decisions for change were made by others and forced upon them.

6   *For gathering, processing and disseminating information* A committee may be formed to undertake these functions and so provide a vital co-ordinating link between departments. The role of the Safety Committee in an organisation, composed of members from each department, is a useful example.

7   *To evaluate and analyse past decisions or events* A committee may be set up to evaluate performance and to initiate inquiries/investigations/reports.

It is important to remember that a group is made up of individuals, and that some conflict might arise between the individual's interests and group or organisational interests. For example, a group decision to restrict overtime working might severely affect an individual's income. This is a very basic example, but studies have been made which identify the situation where individual and organisational objectives are the same, and situations where they conflict. One of the classic investigations is the Hawthorne study for which research was carried out at the Hawthorne plant of Western Electric, in the USA. The study demonstrated that higher output could be achieved where objectives coincided, and conversely that output could be held back if there were conflicting interests. The following two extracts show how the complexities of group dynamics can control relatively simple situations.

Extract A

One of the most famous studies carried out at the Hawthorne plant was the lighting experiment. Here the researchers chose a group of workers working on a large production line producing components. The workers were re-allocated to a small production line where the conditions of working could be easily altered and their individual output measured. The components were small and it was thought that by increasing the level of lighting the working conditions would be improved. Consequently, the lighting was upgraded in stages and the group's reaction measured at each stage. With every increase in lighting there was an increase in output. With further reductions to comparatively low lighting levels the output remained high. Apparently the increase in output was due more to the presence of the experimenters than the lighting levels. The experimenters had created unique conditions where, for once, the workers regarded themselves as a 'special' team and they discussed the work amongst themselves with great interest. This introduced new factors of motivation such as pride in the job, which were not present before. It could be said that the external physical conditions were less important than the new values of the team. The result was an increase in output becoming the common objective shared by the team and the management.

It would be wrong to suggest the experiment showed that changes in physical conditions had no effect on the output. However, it seems evident that the group was motivated by the very fact that it was an experiment. This shows the need for careful structuring of experiments and the necessity for control groups in which conditions are not altered. General research shows that under carefully controlled conditions there are optimum levels of lighting for work done under a variety of conditions. Moderate levels are sufficient for reading tasks whereas high levels are needed for activities such as surgery.

Extract B

A group of workers at the Hawthorne plant were secretly observed while they worked wiring components together into large installations for telephone exchanges. The workers were paid a bonus based on the efforts of the group as a whole. However, it was soon clear that the workers, although they may have wished for a larger bonus, commonly agreed a restriction in output. This represented the group collective view of 'a fair day's pay for a fair day's work'. Norms of 6000 units per day were set as the target for production, but this was less than the group could have produced at full capacity. Anyone who deviated from this target, however, suffered abuse or social pressure from the rest of the group. It was thought that too high an output (and consequent bonus) would make management alter the bonus rates, and to produce too low an output was unfair to others in the group.

It seems that the group objectives were not to seek high levels of productivity, which the bonus set by management should have produced. The group preferred instead to set their own targets and so brought social pressures to bear on individuals to conform to the group's values. Therefore a group that is cohesive may not necessarily adopt the same objectives as management. The norms, values and customs of the group may be more important to an individual than the extra bonus.

Activity 4

You will need to draw on Units 5 and 6 for this activity. Write a short paragraph in answer to each of the following questions (approximately 10 lines).

1 Why do people join groups?

2 Which do you think are the three most important characteristics of groups, and why?

3 How would you describe the 'perfect' group?

4 With reference to the Hawthorne studies, how many groups can you identify as being in operation, and how would you classify them into types?

5 Selecting any organisation with which you are familiar, identify three separate groups that operate within it and describe each one in terms of its constitution (ie who is in it? – their positions/functions), its purpose, and its success in the context of the organisation.

Unit 7

How groups work

As we have seen, the need to belong to and to be accepted by a group is commonplace, but how do groups work?

- Do they reflect *good* organisation, or do they exist to compensate for *poor* organisation?

- Is there scope for cohesiveness *between* groups as well as *within* groups?

- How far do group or individual objectives line up with organisational objectives?

- What happens inside groups?

The success of any work group depends on effective formation and development. This requires the following:

Identification of roles: members; leader; allocation of work.

Interaction: relationships within the group; relationships with other individuals and groups; common interests and goals; relationship to management; communication patterns.

Cohesion: desire/need to be a member; sharing group goals.

Norms: adoption of informal rules to regulate behaviour.

Effectiveness: level and quality of work/output.

Use of power: co-operating for mutual benefit; neutralising opposition; persuasion; gaining advantage.

The stages of group development are often summarised in the following way, reflecting relatively predictable evolutionary change.

1 *Forming* – the stage at which group members test the group reactions and establish acceptable behaviour and attitudes.

2 *Storming* – this can indeed be 'stormy', as it is the time of negotiation and conflict as power and status are allocated to individuals.

3 *Norming* – the stage at which identifiable group norms start to be established, developing from the 'forming' stage.

4 *Performing* – at this point the group becomes self-managing. Tasks are allocated, leadership established, and everyone knows what their role is, the contribution they can make, and the strengths and weaknesses of other group members.

In the following extract, from a lecture given by the author, you will see how many of the principles of group operation can be seen in informal as well as formal groups. We often find it easier to understand some of the theory when it is related to situations we can readily identify with, so you should find some useful information here on *group size*, *group dynamics* (ie the processes of group behaviour), *group norms* (attitude, behaviour, discipline) and other aspects of group working. Remember, however, that your main concern is with *work* groups, and that you must be able to relate these ideas to work situations.

'One of the first things we have to recognise when thinking about the way in which groups work is that the size of a group will have a direct impact on its structure, nature and effectiveness.

Let's think about a simple social occasion – going to a party. I always like to arrive on time, whereas many people prefer to leave it until a bit later, when things have warmed up. However, getting there early gives me quite an insight into basic group dynamics. When I arrive, there might be three or four like-minded people to whom the hostess can introduce me, and with whom a general conversation will develop. The whole group will probably be involved, and although the subject may change a number of times, everyone will be listening and contributing as the conversation bowls along.

Group dynamics at work in the informal group situation

As more and more people arrive, however, it is impossible to keep "inserting" them into the original group, so individual introductions are made, some people move away, and a number of different groupings will form. The topics of conversation will become more and more varied, and more and more subgroups will evolve.

The principle we need to identify here is that when groups get to a certain size, interaction becomes more difficult, and it often proves more effective to create subgroups in order to maintain the flow of communication.

It is also important to consider the requirements of different character types in this context. In a group of fifteen, for example, a shy person is not likely to have the self-confidence or forcefulness of personality to make himself heard. He may then just become a listener, making little contribution to what is going on. In a group of four, however, there is likely to be much more opportunity for such a person to be drawn in, and encouraged to express his own ideas.

In a situation where an individual is very retiring and adopts a passive, non-contributory role, the group may be losing the benefit of an expert opinion, or a different point of view.

You might be tempted to think from these comments that only small groups can be effective. But consider a different situation: if, in your village, the local community group decided that there was need for an anti-litter day to clean up an area of amenity woodland, would you rather have a large group of people, or just a few to do the work?

To counteract this again, if you have a situation where it is essential to get total agreement amongst a group of people, the larger the group, the more difficult it becomes. If, at work, a task has to be completed which involves a large number of people, the problems of co-ordination are likely to outweigh the benefits of "many hands".

In a large group, it is likely that a structure will emerge – members will adopt particular roles, and rules will develop to help the effective operation of that group. As size increases, so does the need for co-ordination and control, but the opportunity for individual action and initiative can actually decrease, leading to a reduction in satisfaction for some members and a greater danger of conflict.

This appears to be a no-win situation – small groups may be too small to be effective, and large groups can become unwieldy. What we need is an optimum group size for each situation, and this is the task of management. Any well-trained manager will be aware of established research which links levels of absenteeism and staff turnover to the size of work groups, and relates these directly to satisfaction levels amongst the workforce.

An effective management will, therefore, try to create the best-size group for any particular work environment, aiming to maximise efficiency and satisfaction, and minimise absenteeism and staff turnover.

The size of a group, however, is only one of the most basic considerations. In a work situation it is the composition of the group that will have the most significant effect on its operation. The *people* must work well together.

If their basic characteristics and motivation are similar, the group is likely to operate as an effective and stable unit, with little need for overt organisation and co-ordination. On the other hand, if the members of a group have disparate interests and have widely differing characteristics and motivation, it is going to be much more difficult to work as a cohesive unit. Levels of co-ordination and organisation will have to be high, and it is likely that strong leadership will be necessary in order to get anything done.

In a social or recreational group, such as a golf club, there might be such a variety of members that a wide range of activities will have to be available to keep the overall membership satisfied. Some will want mainly social activities; some will be looking for the challenge of the competition; some will simply want to play golf to relax and get some exercise; some will specifically want to improve their game, and will therefore want coaching facilities.

As you can imagine, it is quite likely that in these circumstances sub groups will be formed (committees) to organise and implement the various activities. How much easier it would be if everybody joined simply to play competitive golf. How much more effective a group can be if all members have a common purpose.

As a principle, then, we can say that it is beneficial if group members feel that they have a lot in common, and that whatever the overall aims and strategies might be, all members will support and work towards them. There is nothing more de-motivating than being in a group that is divided and where members seem to be working towards different goals in different ways.

From a management or supervisory point of view, one of the most difficult aspects of groups in the workplace is how to control them. However, all types of group need controlling mechanisms if they are to survive and operate effectively. Now is not the time to move into a detailed study of management styles and techniques, but it is important to recognise that controls must exist.

In most groups the members themselves identify that certain attitudes, values and ways of behaving are expected, and the pressure to conform to these group norms can come from peers or from those in "authority". Sometimes the "rules" are formally documented – as a constitution in a social or recreational club, or as work regulations/working practices in a business organisation. Often they are simply "understood" and accepted as being the right thing to do.

For example, in a college situation it is regarded as unacceptable to "borrow" and use someone else's computer disk, or copy work straight from someone else's disk and use it as the basis for one's own work. This is a moral or ethical norm which has been accepted by most group members. It can also be formally enforced, however, if a tutor identifies that such a practice has taken place. In a work situation it is not uncommon for members of a group to "carry" the workload of an individual who is unwell or under severe stress, thus giving support and aiming to maintain overall group performance.

It is a fact that most people have a need to belong and are therefore willing to conform so that they are not different from other members of the group.

As well as having all the positive characteristics we have talked about so far, a group must support itself if it is to survive. A united front needs to be presented to outsiders and there needs to be cohesion in respect of the principles on which the group is formed. One result of this need for group loyalty is that members' ideas, attitudes, beliefs and actions become more aligned with those of other members. Each member influences and is influenced by others, and there is an ever-present pressure to conform. This all seems quite straightforward – as most theory does – but every person is an individual and has to balance the need to belong against his/her personal ideas and beliefs.

It is quite common for someone to conform through **compliance** when faced with group pressure. This means that they will openly be seen to agree and support group norms in order to gain acceptance. However, such a person might not actually believe in the norms and values, but is prepared to compromise in order to belong. On the other hand, a group member might, after a period of time, come to believe in what the group represents, and therefore "internalises" the group norms as a desirable basis for activity.

Whatever the reason behind it, conformity is a crucial element in group operation, control and survival. Any change from this norm is likely to lead to conflict and possible changes in group membership.'

Conflict We are given a lead-in to some of the problems that can arise in groups in the preceding extract, and so the final part of this unit deals with the idea of conflict – interpersonal conflict, intra-group conflict, and organisational conflict.

From a manager's, supervisor's or leader's point of view, successful 'control' of group activities depends on understanding conflict, identifying the causes, and recognising the tactics and strategies that groups adopt in different situations.

In organisations conflict occurs because of personality clashes, and incompatible pressures or influences. Each member has certain roles, objectives and responsibilities which may be frustrated by others who create barriers and do not co-operate. The results can be varied. Some conflict can be used constructively to create a more dynamic group that is creative, solves problems more effectively, makes better decisions, and is generally more productive.

Unfortunately many adverse effects are common, such as high mental stress, unco-operative group behaviour, conflict of goals between the group and the organisation, signs of group disintegration, irrational and illogical behaviour, and breakdowns in communication.

Group versus group
Competition *between* groups can lead to hostility, a reduction of communication, and regression into negative, stereotyped reactions. In the work context, conflict can stem from such things as communication difficulties caused by dissimilarities in work content, problems of co-ordination where there is interdependence in the performance of tasks, and unfair distribution of resources.

Conflict can influence perception, attitudes and behaviour within groups and between groups. Favourable changes may occur if conflict is reduced to a manageable level, and can result in higher productivity and improved working relationships.

However, high conflict levels can cause enmity and sometimes vicious behaviour, for example in sporting activities where players use verbal abuse and even physical violence against each other – and against the referee!

Internal changes
Noticeable changes within a group during intergroup conflict might be: increased cohesion, more autocratic leadership to create high responsiveness, more clearly defined roles, more concern for high performance, stronger loyalty towards the group, discouragement of mixing with 'outsiders', strong control mechanisms for deviation from norms, increased formality, improved co-ordination, and allocation of specific responsibilities.

Changes in group relations
When hostility rises beyond sensible levels between groups, the tendencies are: a decrease in communication, less interaction, distorted ideas about other groups, over-emphasis of enmity, personal or group goals often overriding company goals, and a reduction in opportunities for problem solving and decision making.

Resolving conflict
This is difficult enough if just two people are in dispute, but when groups are involved there is no straightforward solution – there are only 'approaches' which must be tried and applied to situations as they arise.

Some managers prefer *direct action* – changing things at the point of conflict in the hope of wiping out the cause; or bringing the groups together for a structured problem-solving session. Success is not guaranteed!

Another approach can be described as *indirect action* – waiting to see if the problem goes away of its own accord; or improving operating conditions which temporarily alleviate the conflict while an investigation takes place.

A competent negotiator might be able to use his or her skills to defuse the situation through discussion, consultation and persuasion, and thus de-escalate to a point of near agreement. Sometimes, such a person can combine these 'smoothing-over' skills with a degree of shrewd bargaining, and reach a point of compromise.

Combining any of these with positive moves towards increased communication can help create a genuine problem-solving environment.

Other strategies that can be adopted include the following:

- Persuading people that total organisational effectiveness is the overriding goal of all groups.

- Locating and directing energies at a common 'enemy'.

- Identifying a common goal.

- Allocating resources in such a way as to encourage co-operation, eg 'pooling'.

- Avoiding 'win' or 'lose' situations.

- Changing roles within groups.

- Arranging temporary exchanges of members between groups (improves mutual understanding).

Assessment Three Read these notes before you go any further.

Notes 1 This assessment is designed for students attending college, and should be completed by all those on a full-time programme, and by part-time day or evening students.

2 Other students should attempt the alternative assessment.

Read the following case study carefully.

Waterlane College of Higher Education

In any organisation, 'human relations' is an important concept. A fundamental explanation of this term is that it involves the behaviour of both individuals and groups, and, in the context of a working situation, the way in which individuals, factions or departments react to or interact with each other.

Obviously this interaction can have a dramatic influence upon the effective operation of any organisation. Bad human relations can cause delays, lack of co-operation, dissatisfaction and work of a poor standard. The organisational structure of a company is important, and lines of communication and authority need careful planning and consideration.

However, no matter how well-planned and structured an organisation might be, there are no short cuts to effective human relations. When dealing with people's feelings, their status, their sense of security, their personal fears, wants and needs, it is impossible to draw up a set of regulations that will solve all problems that might arise. People, even when they are members of groups, are individuals, and their problems need delicate handling and a sensitive approach. In many circumstances, things can go wrong even when a manager feels every effort has been made to ensure that things run smoothly – as you can see by what happened at Waterlane College of Higher Education.

The background

Within the college, a centralised Office Services section has been established to deal with all the general typing and reprographic requirements of the ten departments. The section has been in existence for 12 months, and was formed by bringing together the old typing-pool and duplicating section. The person who ran the duplicating section retired, and the responsibility for reprography was brought into Office Services under the section leadership of Katherine Standing.

Miss Standing had 'worked her way up' in the college. She had started in the typing-pool at the age of 18 and had proved to be competent and well-liked. After five years she applied for the post of Personal Assistant to the Vice-Principal, Mr W. Farmer, and was chosen from a number of strong applicants. She did the job well and gained valuable general experience of the working of the college and the interrelationships of the various departments. During her ten years as the Vice-Principal's PA, Miss Standing undertook a number of part-time study courses which not only enabled her to improve her skills but also gave her more formal qualifications in office and administrative management. When she was 33 she successfully applied for the post of Supervisor of the typing-pool, and after another few years she became Section Head of Office Services when the section was formed.

She had responsibility for 15 typists and clerk-typists, who were also trained to use the reprographic machinery inherited from the duplicating section. Her main duty was to allocate and supervise work, ensuring that high standards were maintained. Her staff enjoyed working under her, regarding her as firm but fair, and the general efficiency and quality of work was highly regarded throughout the college.

During the last five or six years, Miss Standing took on the responsibility of ordering all the stationery and supplies for her section, and was given authority to assess new products in the office-machine range, which included seeing representatives and demonstrators herself, and subsequently making a report and recommendations to Michael Drysdale, the Chief Administrative Officer. Her recommendations were invariably agreed, and found to be sound in the light of experience.

The first signs of trouble came when the Chief Administrative Officer decided that the reprographic facilities were out of date, and wanted to purchase a sophisticated copying machine which could copy both sides of a sheet of paper at once, collate, staple and virtually operate unattended. He had seen the advertisement for the machine in *Professional Administration* and had contacted the Tamshi company to arrange a demonstration. When John Davey, the Tamshi representative, came to the college he convinced Michael Drysdale that the Tamshi Copyfast was ideal for the heavy copying load of the college. They discussed all aspects of the machines, including servicing, contracts, costs (installation and per copy), flexibility, performance and reliability. When Drysdale was certain that this was the right machine, he called Miss Standing in to talk to the representative. He asked her if she had any queries about the working of the machine or general points she wanted to raise. Miss Standing was surprisingly quiet, asked few questions and seemed not to be interested in the whole business. She did comment, however, that if Mr Drysdale was satisfied then she was sure the machine would be all right.

Putting aside his thoughts about Miss Standing's rather off-hand attitude, Michael Drysdale was able to negotiate very favourable terms with Tamshi, and arranged for the new machine to be installed in three weeks' time. He informed Miss Standing of his decision, and she agreed that she would be present when the Tamshi representative and service engineer came to demonstrate the machine and give her staff basic training in its use. On the appointed day, however, she made it clear that the workload in Office Services was such that she was unable to take time off for the demonstration, and that she could only release seven of her staff for training. She asked her deputy – Joan Waters – to attend in her place. Her general attitude was clearly expressed when she said to Joan, 'All the staff have plenty of experience in reprography, so make sure that not too much time is wasted. All these photocopying machines are very similar, so this training is not really necessary. I certainly hope the machine turns out to be as good as Mr Drysdale thinks – otherwise a lot of time and money will have been wasted.'

The demonstration went ahead, and the machine came into service. Within a couple of weeks problems started to occur. First of all there were some uncharacteristic complaints from departments that work was not being done quickly enough, and in some cases the quality of the copies was not up to standard. Miss Standing explained this away by saying that the machine kept breaking down, and that her staff were finding it difficult to operate. The paper jammed frequently and the toning controls seemed to be ineffective.

When Michael Drysdale heard of the difficulties, he immediately contacted Tamshi and asked for the engineer to call and check the machine. When the engineer came, he found that the basic operation of the machine was quite satisfactory, but that there was evidence of incorrect handling. Paper was being loaded incorrectly, and the automatic controls were being overridden manually, thus causing poor copies. In discussion with Miss Standing he mentioned this, but Miss Standing insisted that the fault was with the machine and that it was certainly not her staff who were to blame. The engineer reported his finding to the CAO and left, confident that all would now run smoothly. Michael Drysdale decided to have a chat with Miss Standing about the situation. He was surprised when he went into her office to hear grumblings and apparent dissatisfaction among the staff, and the general atmosphere was very 'unsettled'. His chat with Miss Standing did not go the way he wanted it to, because she immediately became very defensive and pointed out that neither she nor her staff could be blamed for the malfunction of the machine. She made it clear that there had never been any trouble with the old machines, and implied that she felt he had made a hasty and unwise decision in dealing with Tamshi. The CAO decided to leave things as they were, and, after ensuring that the photocopier was working satisfactorily, said that he was sure there would be no further problem.

Things ran smoothly for the next two weeks, but then the complaints started to come in again. Drysdale was very annoyed about this, and accepted Miss Standing's assertion that the machine was malfunctioning again. He rang Tamshi, and insisted that the problem was corrected.

This time, the service engineer and John Davey, the representative, came along and checked the machine through. John Davey was very puzzled at the problems Miss Standing's section had experienced, but was annoyed to find that there had been further interference with the automatic controls, and that the paper carrier was being over-filled, causing two or more sheets to be taken into the machine and resulting in a 'jam'. The machine was thoroughly serviced, and all the staff were called in to be given individual training in the basics of using it. Many of them seemed to resent being taken away from their 'important' work in order to be shown how to use a machine which was 'not as good as the old equipment'.

In discussion with Michael Drysdale afterwards, John Davey made it quite clear that there was nothing wrong with the machine as long as it was used according to instructions. He felt the staff were 'anti' the machine because of Miss Standing's general attitude, and were making little effort to master the relatively simple processes involved in using it. His impression was that Miss Standing's original lack of interest and subsequent reactions had affected the whole section, and jeopardised a good working relationship between the college and Tamshi.

The CAO was determined to sort the problem out and summoned Miss Standing to a meeting in his office the next day.

Approaching the assessment   This assessment is based on group working, with each group (3–5) members) being established as a working party within Waterlane College of Higher Education.

The Internal Relations Committee of the College consists of senior staff and meets once a month under the chairmanship of the Deputy Director (Personnel), or DDP, to discuss any problems and to work towards more effective personnel policies. As a result of the difficulties in Office Services, he has called for a full report of the situation from each of a number of working parties. The report should analyse the problems, try to identify causes, and try to identify strategies or courses of action which could/should have been taken to avoid the problem. Any suggestions made will have implications for future personnel policy relating to consultation procedures.

This will be a *confidential report* from your working party to the DDP, and will be considered in comparison with reports from other working parties. The main recommendations may be used as the basis for personal interviews with all those concerned. These will *not* be disciplinary interviews.

Task 1   Your working party should produce this as a *memo-report* and ideally it should be in word-processed form. Guidelines on the structure of a memo-report are given in Figure 13. There will be a *single* report from your group.

Task 2   Write a personal commentary on how you feel your working party operated as a group, identifying any problems, explaining how work was allocated, analysing any difficulties (why they occurred) and describing how they were overcome. The aim is to examine the group's performance and analyse your own contribution and impact on the group. A commentary from each member of the group should be attached to the report, and will be used to determine individual grades when averaged with the report.

Note: This is an individual task, and should be completed without consultation or discussion with other group members.

General guidelines   1   You will need to have an initial meeting of your working party to discuss the issues and decide how the work is to be done. Remember, you are submitting a single report from your group. All members will benefit from the grade awarded and should therefore contribute towards its construction. Use your meeting time to decide who is to do what, how the work is to be co-ordinated, what further meetings are necessary, what the agreed approach/solutions/suggestions will be, how the report is to be structured, etc.

2   You may wish to consider the following points as part of your discussion and to help you formulate your ideas:

■   The people who work in Office Services are obviously going through an uncharacteristically bad time. They are getting complaints about their work on the one hand, and being criticised for their general attitude on the other. This obviously leads to low morale, and the situation seems to be going from bad to worse.

Why do you think they have found themselves in this difficult position?

■   Katherine Standing's relationship with management has always been very good in the past. Why does she seem to be in conflict with Michael Drysdale over this issue?

- To what extent do you think Miss Standing can be blamed for the problems her staff have experienced with the new machine?

- What do you think about the CAO's role in this situation?

- If you were Michael Drysdale, how would you approach the meeting with Miss Standing? What would you hope to achieve? How would you deal with her apparent antagonism?

A summary of the general presentation/layout/content of a memo-report is given in Figure 13. Remember that a standard memo heading sequence is required.

TO: .... DATE: ....

FROM: .... REF: ....

Subject/Title

The introductory paragraph has no section heading and will include information on the reasons for submitting the report, the scope, any source material, and how information was collected (if appropriate).

SECTION HEADING

(a) Subheading
  i)
  ii)
  iii)
(b) Subheading
  i)
  ii)
  iii)

Notes: *This main body of the report will be presented schematically under appropriate headings and sub-headings, with numbered points/statements/comments. This does **not** mean that you can write in an abbreviated note form. Grammatical accuracy is important to ensure reader comprehension.*

*The number of sections, subsections and numbered points will depend on the requirements of the question and the complexity of the information you are dealing with. The decision is **yours**.*

SECTION HEADING
(a) Subheading
  i)
  ii)
  iii)
(b) Subheading
  i)
  ii)
  iii)

The concluding paragraph has no section heading and should aim to 'round off' the memo in an appropriate manner. There is no need to summarise your findings, draw lengthy conclusions or make detailed recommendations.

Signature: ....

Figure 13 Guidance on the presentation of a memo-report

Alternative
Assessment Three

Bad Medicine
A case study

Natural Healing Ltd is a producer of a wide range of health products based on pills, capsules, powders, tonics and other medicinal concoctions which are distributed to specialist retail outlets throughout the country, in Europe and other parts of the world. The company has kept at the forefront of technology in the production process, and has a strong Research and Development department. Co-operation between Production and R & D has traditionally been strong, with close relationships developing between the senior staff. The result of this has been an innovative, effective and profitable integration of knowledge and skills.

The policy with NHL is to hold weekly management team meetings in which all functional managers participate, and into which came the new manager of the Packing and Dispatch Department. John West had come from a different type of industry where automated packaging processes were the norm. At this week's meeting he raised the issue of the packing process which seemed to be operating at less than maximum efficiency. He explained the situation:

'The products are packed using production-line techniques where operatives stand at "stations" two metres apart. Here each operative has quantities of a few of the products which they place into boxes that are slowly moving down the conveyor. Sometimes the order attached to the box requires the products handled by a particular individual, and sometimes not. Although this seems quite straightforward, a number of difficulties have developed. Absenteeism is the worst problem and it means either high overtime bills or orders not being available to the customer at the promised time, or both. Discussions with the packers have shown a lack of job interest or boredom which has resulted in mistakes, accidents and suspected sabotage. One day the conveyor ground to a halt, and there was much cheering from the operatives who all sat down on the nearest box and all groaned when the repair was finished. The repair showed that the breakdown was caused by a bolt that had been dropped into the conveyor cogs. Sabotage was suspected but impossible to prove. Statistics show that accidents and mistakes are on the increase. There is a lack of team spirit and the operatives are unwilling to help each other when the occasion arises. They are all paid just the same as others doing the same type of job in the region.'

John West proposed that the production line should be scrapped and that the operatives should work in groups sitting at 'desks', each stocking all of the company's products. Then one packer could complete a whole order for a customer. Small groups could even deal with particular sets of customers whom they might come to consider as 'theirs'. The 'desks' would be arranged so that the packers could see and talk to each other as they worked. The details were not worked out, as John wanted to consult the packers first to seek their active participation in making the change. Some of the managers welcomed the idea but others were unconvinced. There was some opposition to consultation, some scepticism about participation, and a general belief that all the problems could be solved by giving a bonus for better work.

Task 1 Basing your ideas on the information in this section of the text, write a commentary on the groups you can identify in this case study, concentrating on the following aspects:

- identify each group

- identify its function

- explain how it operates

- identify any 'good' aspects of the group operation

- identify any 'bad' aspects of the group operation.

Do not attempt to explain how things could be improved!

Task 2 As John West's assistant, you have been asked to prepare an informal report (memo-report format) summarising his ideas for improving the effectiveness of the packing section, stressing the advantages of group-working for the packers, answering the criticisms put forward by other members of the management team, and forecasting the likely consequence of implementing his proposals.

Justify all your suggestions by reference to the 'theory' of groups outlined in this section. Submit your report to John West.

Unit 8

Developing teams and teamwork

In Assessment Three you approached a real work situation from the point of view of conflict, group influences, weak management strategies and ineffective human relations – all of which we have seen have a negative effect on working activities. You will, hopefully, have identified some area where use could be made of consultation procedures and positive group dynamics in order to achieve improvements.

We shall now become a little more specific and consider the concept of *teamwork*. A team is a group with a positive cohesiveness and a requirement to work together to achieve specific goals – often it is created specifically to perform certain tasks, and the formation, development and successful operation of the team can therefore be seen to conform to certain criteria. In other words, a team isn't just 'formed', it is *built*.

Many opportunities for team creation will occur naturally, because of the functional areas/groupings in which people work – eg a central typing-pool, an accounts section, a print room, etc. However, these natural groupings do not mean that the members *operate as a team*. A team is created from a group, and it is usually the supervisor's or manager's job to ensure that this happens. There are certain basic principles which can be applied to summarise the team leader's general responsibilities, and these are that he or she should ensure:

1   objectives are set

2   work is completed on time

3   standards are maintained

4   work is co-ordinated

5   team members work well together

6   the team is kept up to date with relevant information

7   problems are solved and decisions made

8   discipline is applied where necessary.

Obviously, this is not as easy as it sounds, and any team leader must constantly monitor and be aware of how the team is performing. As well as the general organisational requirements outlined above, a team leader (whether the team exists because of functional activities or is set up to perform a specific task) has other aspects to consider if maximum effectiveness/efficiency is to be achieved. These are:

- the needs of the team
- the needs of individuals
- the needs of the organisation (the job or the tasks).

The team

People work together much more effectively if morale is high and there is a good team spirit. The leader can encourage this by:

- selecting staff with the right mix of skills and personalities to enable them to work harmoniously together
- encouraging ideas and suggestions
- making use of people's strengths
- involving the team in decision making
- dealing with grievances promptly, representing the team to a higher level of authority when necessary
- distributing work fairly
- keeping the team properly informed by instruction and briefing meetings.

In addition, the physical and general work environment is important for the well-being, safety and health of team members. Therefore action should be taken to:

- make adequate safety and first aid provision
- provide training where necessary
- consult members on safety matters
- conduct regular safety checks of equipment, plant and buildings
- ensure that emergency drills are implemented regularly
- encourage good practices.

The individual

Each team member is an individual, with his or her own thoughts, ideas and interpretations, but most people will enjoy being a member of a team if they are fully involved and fully aware of what is going on. Again, it is the team leader's responsibility to disseminate information and ensure that each team member knows:

- what the team is trying to achieve

- what is expected of him or her

- to whom he/she should report and for what he/she is accountable

- the level of performance expected

- the progress he or she is making.

It is also quite important to recognise that nobody wants to lose their individuality or identity just because they are a member of a team, and therefore opportunities should be made to:

- listen to individual problems

- provide individual counselling where necessary

- visit and talk to each individual as they work

- conduct appraisal of individual performance

- give regular opportunities for consultation and feedback on aspects of appraisal.

As you can see, the team leader has a substantial job to do, and yet another crucial element of this role revolves around motivating staff. The whole concept of motivation is quite complex, but certain basic strategies can establish a sound base from which to work. For example:

- consulting with staff for opinions and advice

- giving constructive criticism

- giving staff credit for good ideas – and using them

- being fair and impartial

- training and developing staff for promotion.

The job – the needs of the organisation

The whole purpose of a team is to do a job, and to do it well – but this does not just happen. It requires planning (ie what, why, when, where and how the job is to be done), and monitoring of performance (to identify variations in output, breakdowns, delays, errors, bottlenecks, wastage, good practice, etc). Monitoring can be done in a number of ways ranging from the informal (chatting to people on the job, observing, wandering around) to the formal (quality sampling, logging of output, appraisal of staff performance). There might even be scope for an 'Organisation and Methods' investigation, but this is not usually introduced as a normal part of team working.

Activity 5

Using your own work experience as the source (current or previous), write a commentary on the monitoring processes that have been applied to you/your work, and assess their effectiveness in the context of your own and your work group's/team's performance.

You should start by describing briefly the job or team activities on which you are basing your commentary, and then identify each monitoring process under a subheading, explaining how it operated, who was involved, how you were affected, what the outcomes were.

Some possible monitoring processes are given on previous pages, and below:

Staff appraisal

Observation

Informal interviews

Quality control/sampling

Reviews (PERT – Programme Evaluation and Review Techniques)

Monitoring of output levels (productivity)

Target setting

Consultative meetings

Staff training seminars

Note: There is more detailed information on monitoring, control and quality assurance in Section Four.

We have looked at how teams can be formed, encouraged, managed and monitored, but we haven't yet given much consideration to how individuals operate in a team, what roles they take on, and how their attitudes affect their work and relationships.

In a formally constructed team (eg a working committee), roles can be easily identified such as Chairperson, Secretary, Treasurer; but it is the informal roles adopted by individuals within groups and teams which can be significant to the success of the 'body'. If a leader is not formally appointed, one will undoubtedly emerge, as the successful operation of the team will demand this. There might also be the 'short-circuiter', who cuts corners in order to speed the process; the innovator, who always comes up with new ideas or new ways of solving problems; the worker, who is always willing to take on extra work and carry out decisions made by the rest of the team;

the 'yes-man'; the walking 'rule-book'; the loner; the team worker or conciliator, who is skilled at calming people down, smoothing things over, negotiating compromise and managing the human relations in the team; the resource investigator, who keeps the team in touch with others in the organisation.

Clearly a variety of people with a range of skills can mean that a team is versatile and dynamic, and the complexities of team structure are deepened by the complexities of individual attitudes and behaviours.

Personal attitudes to work vary enormously. Some people can be relied upon to produce work that is always of a high standard and completed within the time stipulated. Others are over-conscientious and whilst their work contains very few errors, it takes them too long to do it and slows down production. Some people get a sense of achievement from completing as much as possible; they get through a large volume of work and speed up the general pace, but often make errors in the process which have to be checked and corrected.

Attitudes towards other people also vary. Some people work happily in a team, doing their share and lending a hand when others are overloaded; they are willing to work late to get jobs finished and make sure no one else's work is held up. Others prefer to work independently and whilst their work may be of an excellent standard, they resent being tied to the pace and needs of other workers and often resent authority as well, sometimes making decisions beyond their terms of reference. Just as difficult to cope with are the people who refuse to display any initiative and only do what they are asked to do or are lazy and do as little as possible.

A manager or supervisor must recognise that all individuals are unique and that just because they work together does not necessarily mean they share the same needs, ambitions, attitudes or outlooks. Personality traits which cannot be changed must be accepted and used to the advantage of the group. The group itself will, in any case, exert its own pressure on members who do not conform to its code of behaviour, and this often proves more acceptable and effective than intervention by the superior.

Activity 6

Using the information you have dealt with in Section Two as a starting point, and drawing from the case studies described in the text and the assessments, explain what you understand by the following terms:

(a) *Relating to working practices*

   i) protectionist
   ii) defensive
   iii) aggressive
   iv) proactive

(b) *Relating to individuals' roles within groups*

   i) team workers
   ii) innovators
   iii) chairperson
   iv) team leader
   v) catalyst

You may find it helpful to do a little further reading/research before completing this activity, and if you are college-based it could be useful to discuss the activity with colleagues in order to help you clarify your ideas.

Assessment Four

Jobbies

'Jobbies' was set up as a personnel agency five years ago with two partners, Dianne Warmer and Jessica Willey. After a difficult couple of years, the business began to grow, and when the opportunity came to purchase the ground floor of the building in which they had started the business, the partners decided to buy it and open an office services bureau as an adjunct to the agency. Dianne would run the agency, and Jessica the office services bureau.

The business was still run as a single entity, with two identifiable sections:

Partners: Dianne Warmer and Jessica Willey
Secretary: to both partners – Stacey Fox

Personnel Section
Manager/Partner: Dianne Warmer
Personnel Officer for Office Temps:
Philippa Johns – responsible for one assistant
Personnel Officer for Industrial Temps:
James Cook

Personnel Officer for Permanent Staff:
Peter Child
Administrative Officer: Katie Matthews – responsible for:
   one accounts clerk (full-time)
   one wages clerk (part-time)
   one receptionist (who liaises with the Secretary)
Publicity and Sales Officer: Pamela Wendle

Office Services Section
Manager/Partner: Jessica Willey
Sales Supervisor: Joan Johnson – responsible
for:
    one sales assistant (full-time)
    one sales assistant (part-time)

Reprographics Operator
Telex/Word Processing Operator (who liaises
with Secretary)
Computer Operator

Note: You are advised to read the first part of Unit 12 in Section Four, and look at Activity 12 before attempting this assessment.

The situation now

You have recently been promoted from the post as Computer Operator to the post of Sales Supervisor. The vacancy occurred because of a dispute between Joan Johnson and the partners, which resulted in her dismissal. There was some bad feeling over this at the time amongst the staff in Office Services, but after chatting with some of them you decided to apply for the post. There was some surprise when you were actually appointed.

Now you have been doing the job for just over a month, some problems have arisen. You have experienced a lack of co-operation from the sales assistant since your promotion and you suspect that the other staff have some doubts about your abilities. You knew that things might be difficult at first but expected the situation to have improved by now. Instead, you seem to have a backlog of work waiting to be done. Jessica Willey is concerned because orders are taking longer to complete, the reprographics operator has threatened to hand in her notice because she is overworked even though the part-time sales assistant often doesn't have anything to do, and you are having to operate the computer as well because the person you appointed three weeks ago is now on three weeks' holiday. Jessica Willey has asked to see you today to discuss the problems and you anticipate she is having second thoughts about promoting you.

In order to rationalise your ideas before this meeting, you decide to sit down and write some notes to help clarify your thoughts. You jot down the following headings and then start to write out the answers.

1   Why am I in this mess?

2   Why was I appointed? Why was I chosen for the job?

3   Was I properly prepared for promotion? Did I need special training?

4   Should management have anticipated the situation and taken action?

5   Is internal promotion a good idea?

6   What action will I take to improve the situation?

7   What have I learned from my mistakes?

Task 1   Draw up an organisation chart and try to show clearly functional, line and staff relationships (see Figure 14 on page 66 for a revision sheet on these relationships, and Figure 15, page 67, for a specimen organisation chart). If you feel there is scope for re-organising the business to rationalise the functional areas, draw your chart to reflect this. On your chart write notes to explain one functional, one line and one staff relationship.

Task 2   Produce answers to the questions presented in Task 1, giving full explanations and reasons where appropriate. Where possible you should relate your answers to the work on groups and team building that you have dealt with in this section, and indicate clearly how any of the principles could have been applied to avoid the problems, or could still be applied to overcome/prevent current/future difficulties.

Notes   Some of the concepts you may wish to consider in relation to this task are summarised below. However, the list is not exclusive or exhaustive, and you should be prepared to introduce other ideas if you think they are relevant. You will need to read through Section Two again to refresh your memory on how these concepts relate to business situations.

■   A supervisor also needs to be a team leader.

■   A group is not automatically a team.

■   An effective team does not just happen – it has to be built.

■   An effective supervisor must be aware of his/her responsibilities as a team leader.

■   Poor planning and co-ordination of work leads to inefficiency.

■   Objectives must be identified and recognised.

■   Effective consultation procedures and regular briefing/planning meetings are important.

■   Problems should be quickly identified and addressed.

■   Problem solving is often easier if staff are involved (co-operative/participative management).

■   Any manager should be able to discipline staff effectively, without conflict.

■   There should be a balance between the needs of the team, of the individual and of the organisation.

- 'Conflict' situations and the problems they can cause should be recognised (eg high stress levels, unco-operative group behaviour, breakdowns in communication, hostility, negative reactions).

- Appropriate strategies need to be adopted to deal with problem solving and resolution of conflict.

- Motivation of staff is important.

- Training needs should be identified.

(a) Line relationship

This is a relationship which exists between a senior and his/her subordinate at any level of the organisation. For example, in Rayco Ltd (see Figure 15), such a relationship exists between the Production Director and the Production Manager, and between the Works Manager and the Assistant Works Manager.

(b) Functional relationship

This is the relationship which exists between those holding functional (or specialist) posts and those with direct executive responsibilities. For example, in Rayco Ltd the post of Personnel Director is a line management post only in the sense that the holder has authority over the staff in his own department. His main function is to advise and assist all the other departments on personnel matters. Because he is an expert in his field he is also empowered to make rulings which must be complied with by staff over whom he has no direct line authority. If, for example, the Personnel Director has grounds for refusing to recruit a particular job applicant (because, possibly, of poor references), his authority for recruitment will override the line director's responsibility for selection.

(c) Lateral relationship

This is the relationship between personnel working at the same level – that is, none is superior or subordinate to others. In Rayco Ltd such a relationship exists between the Production Manager and the Works Manager.

(d) Staff relationship

The word 'staff' here is used in the sense of a support (as in 'wooden staff'). Such a relationship occurs, for example, between a Managing Director and his/her personal assistant. The holder of such a post has no formal relationship with other persons within the organisation, nor does he/she possess authority in their own right. This kind of relationship exists between the Managing Director and the Company Secretary in Rayco Ltd.

(e) Span of control

The number of people who are *directly* accountable to the same person constitutes the 'span of control' of that person.

Figure 14 Relationships in a business organisation

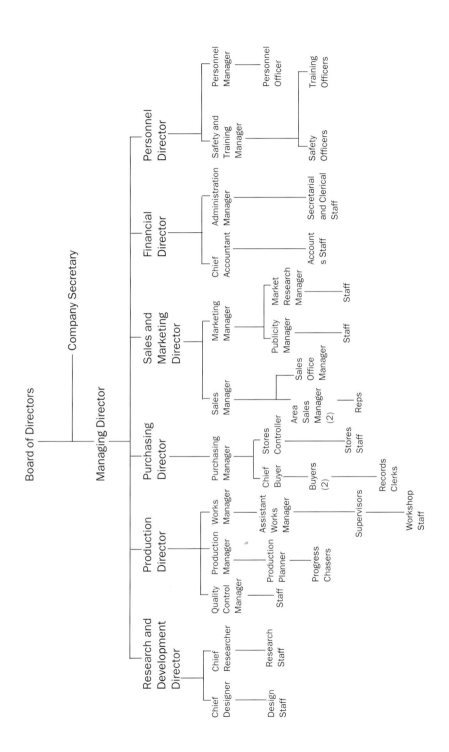

Figure 15 Organisational structure of Rayco Ltd

Management, leadership and communication

Unit 9

You will already have some ideas about the distribution of authority in an organisation, and at the end of Section Two you will have seen the use of organisation charts as an attempt to illustrate the formal relationships in an organisation, the main lines of communication, and the flow of authority and responsibility through various levels of management. Now it's time to look at 'management' as a concept, and to think about the different interpretations that can be applied to such a commonly used word.

How often have you heard (or made) statements like:

'It's a management decision.'
'They went bust because of poor management.'
'It's management's responsibility to deal with that problem.'

In general terms, 'management' refers to a collection of people who are responsible for running a business on behalf of the owners: that is, they establish and implement policy, and aim to ensure profitability. In a practical business situation, all sorts of terms are used to describe people at different levels who are considered to have management responsibilities, the most common ones being *executive*, *administrator*, *supervisor*, *director*, and, of course, *manager*. These terms are often used very loosely, with the functions and responsibilities associated with a particular title differing from organisation to organisation.

Office work is particularly difficult to classify and define, so to get some idea of where any individual could fit into the hierarchy, it can be useful to construct a diagram showing what skills and qualifications might be required at particular levels (see Figure 16). This pyramid structure also indicates that the higher up the 'ladder' you go, the fewer people there are holding those responsibilities. An indication is given in the diagram of the number of staff who might be working at each level in a hypothetical medium to large company.

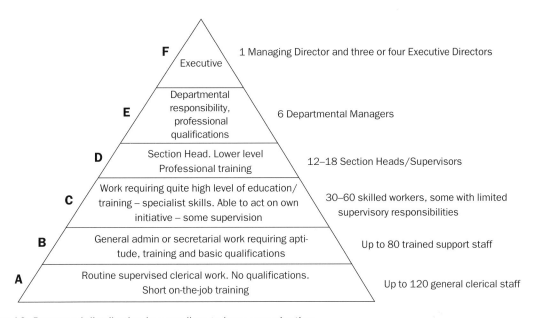

Figure 16 Personnel distribution in a medium to large organisation

Management styles

Having thought about the levels of authority outlined in Figure 16, you should be able to demonstrate fairly clearly what you think a manager is. The next stage is to look at how managers work. How do they deal with people? How do they solve problems? How do they get things done? What styles of management do they employ? Is a manager automatically a leader?

Obviously, each individual will react to situations in different ways, and a manager is no different. However, there are some broad classifications that we can use to show how different approaches can be adopted and identified as styles of management. The diagrams in Figure 17 show some of the characteristics of these styles.

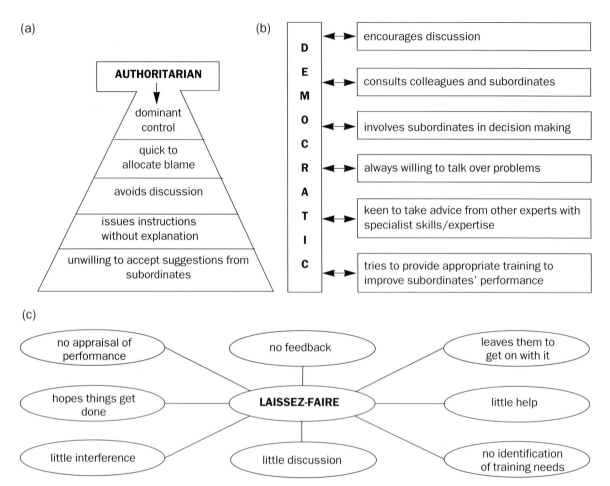

Figure 17 Three styles of management: (a) authoritarian (b) democratic (c) laissez-faire

In the working situation, each of these styles is quickly recognised by members of groups and teams, who can react in ways that are not always beneficial to the organisation. For example, the *authoritarian* approach can work in situations where staff are inexperienced or where quick decisions need to be made, but it can cause resentment where consultation is needed, or where the manager is dealing with people who have particular expertise.

The *democratic* manager, on the other hand, involves the group in decision making by explaining the problems and the factors involved and then asking them to contribute to the discussion and to make the decision; it might even be appropriate to ask them to investigate and define the problem. There must be a willingness to delegate and to modify views. This style is appropriate when negotiating or trying to solve complex problems, where consultation is needed and where expert staff are available and willing to take responsibility. It is not appropriate for use with inexperienced staff, where procedures are already established, or where quick decisions are needed.

The *laissez-faire* manager is not really a manager at all, because he/she is likely to be out of touch with members of the 'team' (if they can be called a team). The laissez-faire manager is likely to be involved regularly in 'crisis' or 'reactive' management – ie he/she leaves things alone until they go wrong, and then panics in order to put things right!

One further classification which is sometimes identified is the *paternalistic* manager. He/she does ask for opinions but then makes the decision and persuades the team to accept it. Although some work is delegated, there is not always a willingness to delegate the necessary authority with it. This approach works with staff who have limited experience, and enables decisions to be made quickly, but it should not be used when competent and expert staff are available because they become frustrated when their skills are not fully recognised and used.

There is no 'best' style of leadership that will automatically lead to high work performance or ensure long-term morale. Democratic styles tend to increase job satisfaction and group cohesiveness, but some employees prefer more direction and do not want to be involved in decision making.

Whatever style is adopted, the leader must ensure that the needs of groups, individuals and the task itself are balanced and considered. If there is a total concentration on the task in hand without considering the needs of people, then morale (and co-operation) will fall. Also, if individuals cannot see the results of their efforts, there will be no sense of achievement.

The manager

When trying to identify the personal qualities we would associate with someone in a management position, it is likely that most of us would expect to find intelligence, a sound knowledge of the business, good general and professional qualifications, proven expertise in a specialist area, effective communication skills, an ability to get on with people, and the confidence to make decisions. A manager with such personal qualities should have no need to adopt one particular style of management, because he or she will recognise that every situation requires a different approach: sometimes the work will get done more effectively if people are left to get on with it;

sometimes, in a crisis, it will be necessary to override normal consultative procedures and implement an immediate course of action.

The skill of management is to read a situation accurately, and to adopt an approach that is most appropriate in the circumstances, and will achieve the best results. In achieving these results, the manager has to rely on the staff, and accept responsibility for the quality of their work. Obviously it is in any manager's best interests to ensure that the people under him or her are working as well as they can, and performing their jobs effectively. In order to monitor these aspects of a department, some system of appraisal is essential, whereby each individual can be made aware of his or her performance and progress. One method of doing this is by implementing a policy of *management by objectives* (MbO).

How MbO works

The essence of this system is that the organisation has to identify and establish exactly what it intends to achieve over the next 'period' (the period can be six months, twelve months or sometimes longer). These overall objectives will require a particular approach if they are to be achieved, and within an organisation a forward-planning team needs to establish how the various departments have to work to help achieve the objectives, and what specific contribution each can make to the overall plan. This process should involve consultation with department managers and result in the establishment of a set of departmental objectives for each functional area.

Logically, this process can be continued down through the organisation so that the various subsections within each department can be examined to see how they can help the department meet its objectives, and individuals in responsible positions can – through discussion and consultation, participation and involvement – establish with their supervisors an appropriate and feasible range of personal objectives. This may involve analysis and re-drafting of job descriptions, and highlight a need for specialist training.

One thing to bear in mind about an MbO approach is that, at the individual level, the objectives identified are likely be quite specific in their requirements. As you move up through the organisation to identify departmental objectives, branch objectives and corporate objectives, they will be formulated in much more general terms, with overall policy statements indicating broad plans of action rather than specifying particular achievement or training criteria for individual employees.

However, it is at the individual level that the work has to be done, and the principles of MbO imply a regular system of consultation and appraisal for all employees. Implemented effectively, MbO can lead to the motivation and development of individuals through regular and systematic reviews of performance, the identification of training needs, the co-ordination of effort, and (hopefully) the achievement of the organisation's goals. However, effective implementation needs to be based on a participative approach rather than an authoritarian one, and consultation, performance review and appraisal can be very time consuming for a busy manager.

Activity 7	Consider this conversation between two senior managers concerning the introduction of a formal system of appraisal into their company. John Reaper is the Production Manager, and Angela Dunsford is the Personnel Manager.

JR: I don't see the point of introducing these appraisal procedures if we know our staff well, and know what they can do. It's a waste of time and money.

AD: The main point is, John, that it would benefit the company as well as the individual. It's not a one-sided thing and it can lead to a much more effective use of our main resource – people!

JR: Sounds like a lot of nonsense to me. All my people are interested in is how much they can take home at the end of the week.

AD: I agree that salary is certainly an important element, and this would be considered as part of any appraisal system. The aim, however, would be to make sure staff are aware of the *basis* for awarding salaries, and to establish a direct link between performance and reward. It's much better that people know where they stand – but salary isn't the most important thing . . .

JR: You try and tell my staff that!

AD: OK! Let's look at it from the production

point of view. If your staff were paid according to the quantity or quality of work they produced in any period, what would their reaction be if they suddenly found their wages were £20 less than normal one week?

JR: They'd be knocking on my door for an explanation.

AD: Exactly! They would want to know what had gone wrong, or where *they* had gone wrong. This is a basic function of formal appraisal schemes – to identify strengths and weaknesses. Then, if anybody has a particular talent, it can be exploited; or if the employee has shown that he or she is weak in any particular area, appropriate guidance or training programmes can be designed to remedy this. The company and the worker benefit by making the worker more efficient.

JR: Well, it sounds all right in theory, but you've used a rather extreme example . . .

AD: All right, let's think of another situation. What if someone on the production line came up with an idea for improving the process and saving time and materials in making a particular component?

JR: They'd probably tell the Chief Engineer, who'd discuss it with me, and if it proved practical we might implement it. If it did work, the 'inventor' would get the standard £50 bonus.

AD: That's all right in the production area, but how do you identify 'potential' in other areas such as clerical or administrative or executive?

JR: I hadn't really thought about it.

AD: One of the ways is to have regular discussions with people and encourage progressive thought by openly discussing how jobs are done and what the problems are. Individuals can be assessed in this way, and given tasks to do which allow them to develop their own skills and potential. It's not so cut-and-dried as your production solution, but often the only way to get the best out of people is to give them a little more responsibility, provide incentives, and enable them to take on more challenging work so that they can prove their abilities. The appraisal interview can be the springboard for this sort of action.

JR: Well, that certainly seems to make sense, and I suppose it's one way of getting to know your staff a bit better. In fact, it could be a useful two-way communication exercise, giving the staff the chance to talk about any worries or complaints that they might have as well as trying to assess their strengths, weaknesses and potential.

AD: Now you're talking! That's exactly the way I would hope an appraisal system would work . . .

JR: You hold on a minute! I didn't say I accepted the whole idea, just that I could see some useful possibilities . . .

AD: Well, let me put some other ideas to you. You know we all work to the MbO system of setting goals or targets for each six months? The appraisal system can be integrated with that and used as a means of discussing and establishing individual and departmental goals for the next period. This would then tie in very nicely with the overall staff planning policy, and we could ensure that everybody is – as far as possible – being employed in the most efficient and cost-effective way.

JR: Some of this seems a bit airy-fairy to me, but I can certainly see the usefulness of some aspects of a formal appraisal system. I'll have to think about it a bit more. Let's have another chat before Friday's board meeting.

Task   Taking the preceding conversation as the springboard for your ideas, use a table like the one opposite to outline the aims and benefits of an effective appraisal scheme. You can make use of any other source material you can find, but don't be tempted to give lengthy descriptions of various methods of appraisal – concentrate on the general *aims* and *benefits*.

There are certain areas you should ensure that you cover, including staff planning (manpower planning), performance assessment and target setting, and you are expected to come up with at least another three aims. For each aim you should summarise the benefits *for the organisation* and *for the individual*.

Aims	Benefits
Performance assessment	
Staff planning	
Target setting	

Unit 10

Leadership and management

The reason for introducing the work on appraisal into Unit 9 is to reinforce some of the ideas dealt with in Section Two, when the responsibilities of a team leader were considered. It is now time to tie up the idea of leadership with that of management, because any effective manager must also be an effective leader.

As we saw in Section Two, good leadership involves:

■ building a team and making sure everyone works together as a team

■ helping people develop as individuals and recognising their different needs and values

■ making sure the job is done properly.

What qualities make a good leader or manager?

In Unit 9 we mentioned general things like intelligence, knowledge of the business, good academic/professional qualifications, etc, but to this we can add some other ideas – see what you think about them:

■ ability to control people

■ ability to analyse situations and think problems through

■ ability to make decisions

■ being prepared to treat people firmly (discipline) but fairly

■ having a sense of humour

■ being willing to co-operate – ie work within a team and with other teams

■ being able to command respect – for technical expertise and/or personal skills

■ being interested in people as individuals and able to identify their strengths and weaknesses

■ being able to give advice without criticising

■ understanding/identifying appropriate training needs of team members

■ being able to plan and organise tasks

■ implementing monitoring procedures, either formally or informally

■ being able to motivate team members and understand the importance/function of motivators.

Identify and write down at least five more qualities that you personally would associate with a good manager/leader.

Delegation It is possible that in your answers you mentioned 'the ability to delegate'. If not, it is certainly an essential technique for any manager to master. Delegation can be defined as 'achieving the organisation's objectives through the work of others', but this doesn't mean simply telling somebody what to do and then forgetting about it. Delegation is a process that demands both parties contributing to the effective completion of the process – see Figure 18.

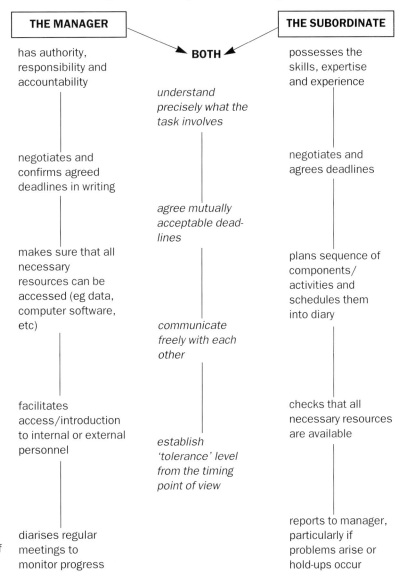

Figure 18 Functions of a manager and a subordinate in the process of delegation

THE MANAGER	BOTH	THE SUBORDINATE
has authority, responsibility and accountability		possesses the skills, expertise and experience
	understand precisely what the task involves	
negotiates and confirms agreed deadlines in writing		negotiates and agrees deadlines
	agree mutually acceptable deadlines	
makes sure that all necessary resources can be accessed (eg data, computer software, etc)		plans sequence of components/ activities and schedules them into diary
	communicate freely with each other	
facilitates access/introduction to internal or external personnel		checks that all necessary resources are available
	establish 'tolerance' level from the timing point of view	
diarises regular meetings to monitor progress		reports to manager, particularly if problems arise or hold-ups occur

Activity 8

As you have seen, the manager/leader must have many qualities and will be involved in a wide range of activities. This activity asks you to consider some general organisational activities that take up much management time, and to come up with some *guidelines for managers* on these topics (Figure 19). Some indication of scope is given in the 'nudge' boxes, but be careful not simply to repeat these ideas. You should aim to give management guidance on how to achieve effective decision making, successful negotiation and resolution of conflict, not just list some of the activities which might be involved. Explain what is involved, and why each particular suggestion could contribute to successful outcomes.

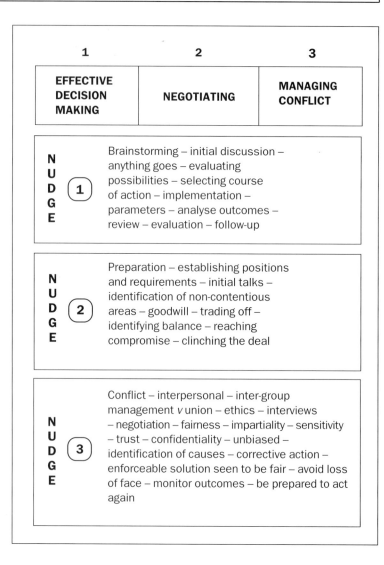

1	2	3
EFFECTIVE DECISION MAKING	**NEGOTIATING**	**MANAGING CONFLICT**

N U D G E **1** Brainstorming – initial discussion – anything goes – evaluating possibilities – selecting course of action – implementation – parameters – analyse outcomes – review – evaluation – follow-up

N U D G E **2** Preparation – establishing positions and requirements – initial talks – identification of non-contentious areas – goodwill – trading off – identifying balance – reaching compromise – clinching the deal

N U D G E **3** Conflict – interpersonal – inter-group management *v* union – ethics – interviews – negotiation – fairness – impartiality – sensitivity – trust – confidentiality – unbiased – identification of causes – corrective action – enforceable solution seen to be fair – avoid loss of face – monitor outcomes – be prepared to act again

Figure 19 Outline of guidelines for managers

Assessment Five   This assessment asks you to think carefully about the skills and attributes you have considered in relation to leadership and management, and apply them to specific individuals. First of all you should select two leaders for whom you have respect/admiration from two different walks of life – eg a sportsman, someone at work, someone in public life. Ideally one should be drawn from a work environment with which you are familiar.

Leaders in government –
Chancellor Kohl of Germany,
and Mrs Thatcher, Britain's
former Prime Minister

Task 1   Write a profile of your chosen leaders according to the following guidelines:

Name: (this can be omitted if you wish)

Job/position/role: (how would his/her job be recognised/identified by an outsider)

Organisation: (name of organisation or indication of main activity)

■   Describe the leadership role which the person fulfils.

■   Identify and describe one situation in which he/she has demonstrated leadership qualities.

■   List the qualities he/she has which make him/her a good leader, and identify those which were required most in the situation above. Explain why.

■   Comment on how other people react/respond to him/her.

■   Identify and describe one situation in which he/she has delegated a task, and analyse how effective the process was.

Task 2   Write a brief commentary on qualities of leadership, using your profiles as examples if you wish, but concentrating your approach on the following aspects:

■   What is a leader?

■   Do all 'leaders' have or need the same qualities?

■   Do leaders need different qualities in different situations?

■   Are leaders born or made?

Unit 11

Communication, people and the organisation

In all aspects of business, people need to co-operate and communicate in order to create and maintain effective working relationships. Free communication flow is the ideal. However, in reality communication is often seen as a downward process whereby 'management' tell 'workers' what to do and what is happening. This attitude can sometimes be reinforced by the misuse, or misinterpretation, of an organisational structure as delineated in an organisation chart. Unfortunately, misconceptions like this can lead to dissatisfaction, an unwillingness to co-operate fully, and unnecessary disputes.

Such an approach to management means that any interference or suggestions from below are resented, there is an unwillingness to confide in 'subordinates', and employees are told only what is essential for them to do their jobs.

Fortunately, the benefits of consultation, participation and person-to-person communication have been recognised and taken advantage of. However, there are still many instances when downward communication is regarded as the norm, with little appreciation of the fact that communication must be a *two-way process* – the person giving the message must be willing to pass on the information (and therefore make a determined effort to overcome misunderstanding, apprehension, antagonism and other barriers), and the recipient must be prepared to listen, think about the information, and reach a point of understanding or agreement with the initiator.

In this context there are many things which can 'block' effective communication. For example:

Barrier	*Possible effect*
language	misunderstanding/ambiguity
intelligence	inability to understand or make oneself understood
suspicion	refusal to 'get involved'
distrust	immediate antagonism
refusal to listen/accept	total breakdown in communication
prejudice	failure to accept logical argument
unsympathetic attitudes	unwillingness to listen to others. inattention inappropriate/incorrect action taken
use of inappropriate medium (eg memo, when personal interview would be better)	no opportunity for questioning/ discussion/further explanation

Activity 9

Other barriers to communication have been identified:

■   atmosphere

■   physical barriers

■   timing

Write a short paragraph explaining what you understand by each of these, and give examples/describe situations in which they could prevent effective communication.

If barriers are not overcome, communication failure leads to conflict and dispute. Therefore although there are always likely to be disagreements in any working environment, there will be less chance of a disruptive 'flare-up' if all employees know what is happening and why it is happening, and are given the opportunity to discuss problems and express their opinions, in the knowledge that their ideas will be listened to.

If communication failure between individuals escalates to the point where it influences the working relationship between groups (eg departments), the effective running of the whole organisation can be affected, with a consequent drop in efficiency, in work flow, profitability and – in the longer term – viability. Some benefits of good communication are shown in Figure 20.

Figure 20 Some benefits of good communication in an organisation

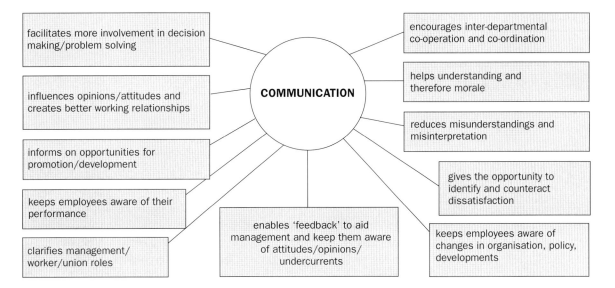

The rumour factory?   No matter what is happening through the more formal communications procedures in an organisation, anyone concerned with administration must be aware of the 'grapevine' – the most informal (and hazardous) route that the information can take.

rumours can spread on very flimsy evidence

used carefully it can be effective

information spreads very rapidly

facts can be exaggerated

important details can be forgotten

facts can become distorted

movement of information cannot be stopped

people believe in it

Figure 21 'The grapevine'

The grapevine reaches all levels of an organisation, and the information is often passed on by people who don't have all the facts, or who might give them a slightly different emphasis to that intended. This doesn't mean that frequent and direct person-to-person communication is always bad: in fact it is accepted as a normal process of keeping people informed of what is happening, and as long as it is used carefully, such informal channels can have advantages. If, for example, an idea or course of action is only tentative, an appropriate rumour fed into the grapevine could provide the opportunity to identify attitudes and observe reactions before making a final decision.

Activity 10 Some ways in which in-company communications can be developed are listed below. Using the organisation chart (Figure 15) on page 67 for reference, consider the overall structure of this organisation, and think carefully about how good relationships and useful communications processes could be encouraged within the workforce. Gather as much information as you can on each of the methods listed below (using a library or any other sources) and consider how appropriate they are, and their implications for the company.

Communication policy at Rayco As a Personnel Officer, and on your own initiative, inform the Personnel Manager of your thoughts and ideas, and recommend what you consider to be the minimum requirements for establishing an effective communications policy. Specify what procedures you consider appropriate, and suggest how any consultative 'groups' should be constituted.

Methods of communication

noticeboard	manager's newsletter
in-house magazine	consultative committee
company newspaper	employee handouts
briefing group	regular person-to-person interviews
suggestion scheme	informal meetings, eg over lunch etc
work directors	union newsletter
appraisal interviews	induction programme
'open door' policy	information sheets
section/departmental meetings	policy meetings

Notes ■ You should consider the needs of new employees, established employees, management, and workers

■ Do not attempt to incorporate all the methods mentioned above. Assume that there are few, if any, formal procedures present, and suggest basic requirements for setting up a workable system, recommending six methods which could usefully and practically be implemented immediately.

Format As this is an internal, person-to-person, self-initiated document, a memo-report format should be adopted.

From the introduction to this unit, you can see that communication is about maintaining and developing relationships. Figure 22 shows some of the relationships with which a manager or supervisor might be involved.

Figure 22 Relationships of a
manager or supervisor

It is fairly clear that the *way* in which we communicate can dramatically affect the response we get, and there are certain techniques
and approaches which can be applied to particular roles/circum-
stances.

Activity 11   You have been asked to give a talk to new employees as part of their induction programme, and the theme is 'Communicating at Work'.

Task   Using the notes below as your guidelines, produce a set of visual aids
which you can use on an overhead-projector in order to demonstrate each
aspect of your talk. You should draw each of these on one side of a sheet
of A4 paper so that they can be photocopied onto a transparency.

Remember: you are trying to produce diagrams, not lists of characteristics.
The diagram will, of course, incorporate adequate written pointers to
enable you to 'talk around' the topic and you can, if you wish, include
simple pictorial material.

You can produce at least one visual aid for each main section if you wish,
or combine the information from more than one section into a single diagram. However, you should produce a minimum of *three* visual aids.

Notes   **A**   *Communicating as a manager or leader*

A manager or leader is required to lead the team to ensure the job is done
as efficiently as possible. This involves communicating decisions, planning
and allocating work, motivating staff, keeping them well-informed and
maintaining standards. So the manager will be involved in:

1 *Giving instructions*

    (a) using clear, concise language
    (b) demonstrating or using diagrams
    (c) encouraging feedback to ensure that the listener has understood

2 *Passing on information*

    (a) changes in policy, plans or work practices
    (b) management decisions

3 *Interviewing and counselling*

    (a) to persuade, explain or encourage
    (b) to assist or give advice
    (c) to discipline
    (d) to reassure
    (e) to appraise performance
    (f) to deal with a complaint

B *Interviewing*

An interview is a face-to-face conversation with a definite purpose.

1 *Planning*

    (a) purpose – why is it necessary?
    (b) content – what will be discussed, in what order?
    (c) place – where will it be held?
    (d) timing – when and how long will it last?
    (e) personality of interviewee:

        (i) how best to approach the individual
        (ii) the degree of formality
        (iii) the tone and style to be adopted

2 *Conducting the interview*

    (a) start the interview by explaining the purpose and setting the tone
    (b) listen carefully
    (c) be flexible by adapting approach according to how interview proceeds
    (d) ask open-ended questions to encourage response
    (e) use body language to convey approval, interest, etc
    (f) close the interview by explaining what has been achieved or what is expected of the employee

After the interview, there should be a follow-up to ensure any action agreed has been carried out.

C *Communicating upwards*

The role of a subordinate is to assist by carrying out instructions effectively, by being resourceful and showing initiative. This can involve:

(a) accepting requests courteously and without argument
(b) listening and giving feedback to show understanding
(c) anticipating likely questions and having answers ready
(d) offering suggestions or help
(e) making constructive criticisms of current or proposed systems and procedures

D *Communicating with a group*

1 *Types of group*

(a) work groups (sections, project teams)
(b) social groups (friends, social clubs)
(c) committees (work-based, voluntary or social)

2 *Group characteristics*

(a) a recognisable identity
(b) a common purpose or goal
(c) a hierarchy which usually includes a leader
(d) a code of behaviour or attitude
(e) control over who should be included/excluded from membership
(f) a united 'front' to outsiders even when there is disagreement internally

3 *Circumstances in which groups need to be addressed*

(a) to launch a new product
(b) to deliver a report to the board, to the shareholders, to colleagues
(c) to instruct trainees on an induction course
(d) to present information to a committee
(e) to address a mass meeting of the workforce
(f) to make an after-dinner speech

4 *Planning*

(a) the purpose of the speech – what are you trying to get across?
(b) the content – what facts are to be included and in what order; how are you going to start and finish?
(c) visual aids – do you need to use OHPs, videos or slides?
(d) accommodation and equipment – check availability
(e) notes – prepare main points of your talk on cards – headings and 'trigger' words are sufficient

5 *Giving the talk*

(a) start with the purpose of talk
(b) use brief notes for reference
(c) speak clearly
(d) keep to the time allocated
(e) use visual aids

(f)   use non-verbal signals (facial expression, eye contact)

(g)   vary the pitch of your voice

(h)   end with a summary or an indication of action required

E   *Listening*

Any manager will spend much time (up to 50%) listening – but how many are good listeners? This valuable interpersonal skill is one that everyone should try to develop.

1   *Reason for listening*

(a)   to obtain information

(b)   to understand the ideas, attitudes and feelings of others

2   *How to improve your skill*

(a)   actively concentrate

(b)   ensure there are no interruptions

(c)   avoid distractions such as noise

(d)   maintain eye contact and use body language

(e)   ask 'open' questions ('Tell me about . . .')

(f)   request facts

(g)   ask 'probing' questions ('Can you give me an example?')

(h)   give encouragement (smiles, nods, leaning forward)

(i)   repeat complex ideas for clarification/comprehension

3   *Benefits of effective listening*

(a)   finding out information

(b)   discovering how people think

(c)   improving relationships

(d)   improving morale

(e)   getting fresh ideas

(f)   identifying (and solving) problems

F   *Non-verbal communication*

In the interpersonal context, this means 'body language', and includes all sorts of gestures, expressions and movements:

(a)   shaking hands; hand on shoulder; slap on back

(b)   folded arms; leaning forward; hunched up; laid back

(c)   direct eye contact; looking away; wide/narrow eyes; frowns; raising eyebrow; tapping feet; drumming fingers; mouth movements; nose movements

G   *Written communication*

1   *Internal*

(a)   Memos – used for upward, downward or horizontal communication; standard heading sequence, often to individual design of the organisation; no salutation or subscription; usually initialled rather than signed.

(b) Summaries/abstracts – presentation of important information in condensed form; saves time and easy to assimilate; requires high level of skill to understand a wide range of information, identify key points, analyse complex issues, retain objectivity.

(c) Reports – present information in a logical format for the recipient to use as the basis for decision making; can be purely information (presentation of facts) or advisory (presentation of facts plus recommendation or conclusion); various types include short formal, short informal, memo-report, extended formal; layout and presentation usually schematic, giving logical development of ideas and findings; the written style should be abstract and objective, with no personalisation; any report must fulfil the 'terms of reference' – ie the statement of what is required or is intended.

(d) Notices and bulletins – these are general, 'open' forms of communication, often posted on a board or distributed to all staff.

(e) VDUs and 'hard copy' – screen-to-screen messages can be sent between terminals, and printouts can provide confirmation if required.

2 *External*

(a) Letters – probably the most widely used method of external communication; wide variety of functions; layout and style is important as it reflects the company image and the 'quality' of the sender; any letter should be carefully planned, logically structured, concise, clear and unambiguous.

(b) Telex, telegrams, fax and electronic mail – normally used for urgent written messages or copies of documents; quite expensive; should be as concise as possible.

(c) Advertisements/notices – usually issued through the medium of the press; need to be attractively designed with effective layout for maximum visual impact; quite expensive; language should be simple and concise; aim is to attract attention.

(d) Press releases – normally issued to the media to publicise important events, changes in company policy, new contracts, successful expansion or deals. Formal structure and conventions should be followed. Information should be relevant to intended audience, concise and precise; should be written in the 'third person' – ie an abstract style.

Work performance

About Section Four

It is necessary to give a brief introduction to this section in order to clarify what is involved. The syllabus guidelines indicate that you should be able to 'identify factors influencing attitudes and performance at work', and a sound approach to this is to look at organisational structures and the cultures they encourage, motivation, and aspects of group co-ordination, leadership, etc. Some of these topics have been touched on in previous sections, and therefore there is little point in repeating them. This section concentrates on aspects which have not yet been dealt with, but there might be some instances where there is such a degree of overlap that certain principles have to be repeated.

Unit 12

Organisational structures and cultures

Two main characteristics of any organisation are (a) the division of labour, and (b) the distribution of authority. The 'division of labour' refers to the variety of operations that the organisation must carry out in order to achieve its main objectives. The 'distribution of authority' refers to the decision-making apparatus required to plan and control these operations. Both of these characteristics may be shown in an *organisation chart*.

The purpose of organisation charts

An organisation chart can be thought of as a two–dimensional model of an organisation. No such model can effectively convey the reality of executive responsibilities or the complexity of the inter-relationships that exist between the different subsystems. Organisation charts are, therefore, an *attempt* to illustrate the formal relationships in an organisation, the main lines of communication, and the flow of authority and responsibility through all levels of the management hierarchy. Above all, organisation charts provide a complete picture of the organisation in a way that is simple to understand.

Charts are used to show the whole organisation (*system*), the departments (*subsystems*) within an organisation, or details of one department or section only. Some organisation charts concentrate on the functions of the organisation as opposed to the structure of personnel. Certain conventions are normally followed, examples of which are given in Figure 23.

Figure 23 Conventions used in drawing up organisation charts

(a) Formal (line) relationships are shown by a continuous line.

(b) Personnel Officer K Janes — A position or function is clearly labelled or can be enclosed by a box; where appropriate, boxes can contain names as well as job titles. However, this is not standard practice unless a chart is purely for internal use.

(c) ------- Broken lines can be used to denote informal relationships.

(d) 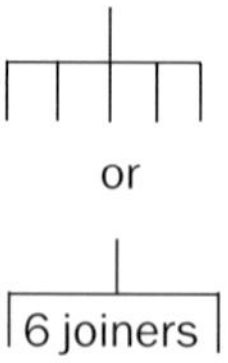 Where practicable the number of subordinates each manager/supervisor has should be clearly shown.

or

6 joiners — If the number is large then figures should be used.

(e) **Key**
red lines – production
green lines – purchasing
A key should be given where appropriate.

Types of organisation chart

Figures 24, 25 and 26 show three different types of organisation chart depicting the structure of a drug manufacturing company, Rayco Ltd, whose main products are toothpaste and anti-dandruff shampoo.

- *Vertical charts or 'T' charts* (Figure 24) are the traditional method – you saw this diagram in Unit 8.

- *Horizontal charts* (Figure 25) are read from left to right and minimise the idea of hierarchical levels.

- *Concentric charts* (Figure 26) are read from the centre outwards, the closeness to the centre reflecting the relative 'importance' of the posts.

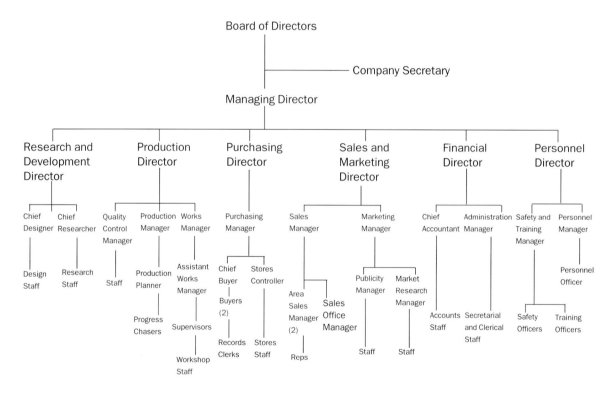

Figure 24 A vertical organisation chart

Figure 25 A horizontal organisation chart

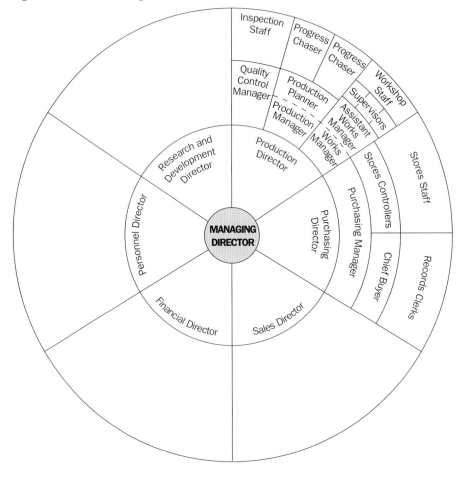

Figure 26 A concentric organisation chart

Molecules versus pyramids

Workers have a much greater say in decisions about their factory or workplace than they used to have. Work has become so specialised that senior members of staff have to trust junior staff who have specialist skills which they do not understand, or have not got time to learn. Therefore all the staff often have to be involved in the decision-making process. To reflect this, as well as to avoid the problems of interpretation previously described, some firms favour a molecular representation of their structure. Figure 27 shows the Marketing Department of a large manufacturing company. The people in the shaded circles all work in Marketing. Those in the plain circles are in other departments, and only part of their work is to do with Marketing. As in other types of chart, where people are joined by a solid line, one is directly responsible to the other. Where people are joined by a broken line there is no direct responsibility, but their work brings them into regular contact with each other.

Figure 27 Molecular representation of the Marketing Department in a large manufacturing company

The interpretation of organisation charts

For simplicity, the following points relate to a vertical chart:

1   *Authority* is the right or power to make decisions or give orders. It flows from the top downwards.

2   *Accountability* is the obligation to follow such decisions or orders. It flows from the bottom upwards.

3   To assume that one post is inferior to another because it occupies a lower level in the chart is incorrect. (This can lead to problems with those who are 'status conscious', and is a recognised disadvantage of vertical charts.)

4   It is important to keep in mind that a chart is only a simplistic model of an organisation, and too narrow an interpretation can contribute to a rigidity of outlook by staff.

Note: The net result of points 3 and 4 above is that many companies deliberately avoid issuing organisation charts to their staff, retaining them for management use only.

Activity 12   Charting the growth of a business organisation

Toms Enterprises

Mr and Mrs Toms buy a shop in Plymouth with a view to selling furniture. After a hectic six months they engage two sales assistants.

Task 1   Chart the organisation (use horizontal charts throughout).

The business goes from strength to strength. Mr and Mrs Toms buy shop premises in Truro and Exeter and take on a manager for each of their three shops, plus four sales assistants (two for each of the new shops).

Task 2   Chart the organisation.

Six months later it's going even better. The Toms employ someone to do their purchasing for the three shops, plus a book-keeping clerk.

Task 3   Chart the organisation.

One year later, and what a year it has been! Mr and Mrs Toms decide that in addition to the furniture from the manufacturers they will market their own. They open a small factory in Bodmin for the manufacture of simple standard ranges of furniture. They employ an experienced joiner as the Works Manager, and 12 additional joiners who are subordinate to him. One of their Shop Managers is promoted to overall Sales Manager, and a further Shop Manager is appointed to fill her previous position.

Task 4 Chart the organisation.

> The furniture being produced by the Toms' factory is 'selling like hot cakes' (because the quality is very good relative to price). Encouraged by their success, Mr and Mrs Toms decide to employ a very well-qualified designer to head a team of three draftsmen and women, so that they can offer a wide range of their own products. They also promote the best joiner to the position of Assistant Works Manager, and engage a further six joiners. Finally, at this stage they decide to put the Purchasing Manager (who will be spending less time buying ready-made furniture and more time buying materials) in a subordinate position to the Works Manager, but of equal status to the new Assistant Works Manager.

Task 5 Chart the organisation.

Task 6 As a company expands, the need for greater specialisation emerges – for example, a separate purchasing department may be set up. Assuming that the Toms' turnover doubles over the next two years, what new specialist departments are likely to be created? Draw up a full organisation chart, showing the structure of the company in two years' time.

Types of organisational structure

There are various ways of describing organisational structures, but many reflect the hierarchical pyramid structure shown in Figure 16 on page 69. The choice of structure usually depends on decisions made by the management team, but in some circumstances the technological or business environment in which the organisation exists can influence how the various elements interact.

Let's start with a relatively traditional structure, which in pyramidical terms can be referred to as a *tall* organisation (Figure 28).

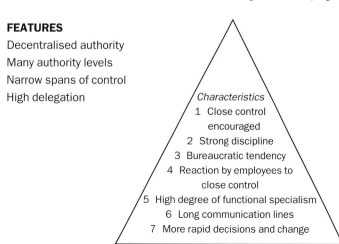

FEATURES
Decentralised authority
Many authority levels
Narrow spans of control
High delegation

Characteristics
1 Close control encouraged
2 Strong discipline
3 Bureaucratic tendency
4 Reaction by employees to close control
5 High degree of functional specialism
6 Long communication lines
7 More rapid decisions and change

Figure 28 A 'tall' organisational structure

This tall form is structured by narrowing the span of control, increasing authority levels, and having a high degree of delegation. Logically, a flat organisation (Figure 29) can therefore be structured by broadening the span of control, decreasing the number of authority levels (cutting down on middle management?), and controlling the extent of delegation.

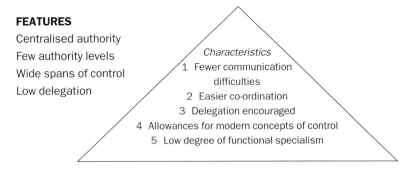

FEATURES

Centralised authority

Few authority levels

Wide spans of control

Low delegation

Characteristics
1 Fewer communication
   difficulties
2 Easier co-ordination
3 Delegation encouraged
4 Allowances for modern concepts of control
5 Low degree of functional specialism

Figure 29 A 'flat' organisational structure

If you study these diagrams carefully, you will probably conclude that there seem to be some inconsistencies, such as in the references to delegation. Bear in mind that simple models like this cannot reflect the complex interactions and activities of individual organisations and, therefore, demonstrate general principles only. For example, there is no mention here of accountability, and it is worth remembering that in loosely structured and controlled organisations, 'delegation' can sometimes be used to 'pass the buck' – that is, push responsibility and accountability on to someone else!

However, this rather cynical observation doesn't affect our recognition of the two different structures.

Activity 13

Looking at the vertical organisation chart of Rayco Ltd, how would you describe the organisational structure? Is it 'tall' or 'flat'? Justify your decision by analysing the organisation chart and explaining why you think it fits into this category. You can draw on any information in this text to support your argument. Do not write more than two sides of A4 paper.

Some organisations, in which the interrelationships and interdependencies between managers are well established and relatively stable, will develop a *matrix structure*. A typical case is where a number of project managers with their own teams are appointed to be accountable for each sector. They are provided with technological back-up from each functional manager who co-operates with them. Thus a complex matrix is formed which not only provides project managers with direct responsibility to the managing director but also collaborative responsibility to all the functional managers.

A simple example is the development of a new specialist car. Project managers for the interior, engine and body will use the resources of the chief designer, production manager and chief engineer. Some criticisms have been directed at this structure, the obvious difficulties being confusion over resource allocation, division of authority, co-operation problems, and divided loyalties.

Being more flexible and more informal, matrix styles suit decentralisation, greater delegation and increased personal accountability. This can cause administration difficulties unless administration is centralised and effective use is made of information technology.

A simple matrix structure is shown in Figure 30.

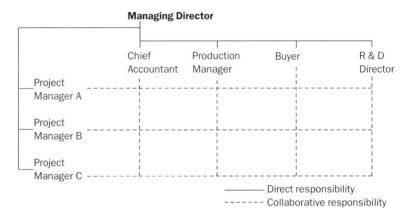

Figure 30 Simple matrix structure of an organisation

Organic structures

One simple way to look at organisations is to see them as a collection of roles which have been established to achieve certain objectives. Organisation charts usually show the formal relations that are supposed to exist between these roles, but we also recognise that numerous informal relationships develop which can have a major impact on the effective operation of the organisation – either a positive or negative impact.

An organic system of management emphasises the use of *all* these relationships, with a definite movement away from traditional static structures. Such a culture is based on effective communication, and must ensure that nothing prevents individuals from requiring/requesting information, advice or additional effort from others. Obviously this means that differences of status, technical prestige, functional 'territory' and privilege must be suppressed, and the communication process must not be concerned simply with the issuing of instructions, the notification of 'happenings' and the basic exchange of information at meetings: it should encourage ongoing consultation and co-operation between people who are working towards the same goals. Rigid job definitions and authority roles give way to a dynamic, more creative environment based on continual interaction between people who work as a team, and the interaction is more lateral than vertical. In simplistic terms, it doesn't matter who you are or what your title is, as long as you can make a positive contribution to the achievement of identified team, group or organisational goals.

As goals change, the roles of individuals adapt to meet the new situation; team constitution might have to alter; responsibilities might be increased or decreased; fresh bases of accountability could be established. In other words, the organisation is a living organism that is constantly evolving to meet the needs of a variety of developing situations, and the requirement of management is to constantly re-examine what the firm is supposed to be doing, with the conscious aim of adapting operating methods and the structure of managerial relationships to its present task. Every effort must be made to encourage the sense of the business as a whole, with objectives and goals common to all its members, rather than a complex of separate jobs.

Mechanistic structures

The mechanistic approach to organisational structure shows a more traditional, hierarchical attitude, with greater emphasis on the line/staff concept, a firm distinction between executive and advisory responsibilities, a clear definition of duties and responsibilities, greater specialisation in management functions, and reliance on formal methods and channels of communication. This type of organisation is easily charted, flexibility is limited, and an overall culture of convention is embedded in the operation.

The problems and tasks facing the organisation are defined and broken down into specialisms which reflect the structure. There is a command hierarchy in which superiors make decisions, issue instructions, regulate operations and control working behaviour. Information flows upwards and downwards, being 'filtered' as it goes up, and 'interpreted' as it goes down. There is little lateral communication, and co-operation/interaction between departments or sections follows procedural guidelines.

In comparison with the organic concept, a mechanistic structure is static, with operations being fitted into the existing structure rather than the structure adapting/evolving to meet the needs of the operations.

In reading these descriptions, you might be tempted to form ideas about which type of structure is 'best', but don't be persuaded into a polarised position. Remember that the qualities of a true manager mean that he/she can identify what is best to meet the needs of his/her organisation, product, customers and workforce. Maybe the decision as to which system is 'best' can only be assessed in the context of success – and how do you define success?

| **Activity 14** | You have recently been studying for a professional qualification in Supervision, and as part of the final assessment you have to take part in a 'viva' (oral examination). The topic you have been given by your assessor is 'Organisational structures and their relationship to management techniques, operational procedures and human relations'. In order to help you prepare for this, draw up a set of notes summarising information relevant to these topics and – where appropriate – showing the relationships between them. You can use a traditional note format with headings, sub-headings and numbered points, *or* diagrammatic presentation(s) – see Figure 31. |

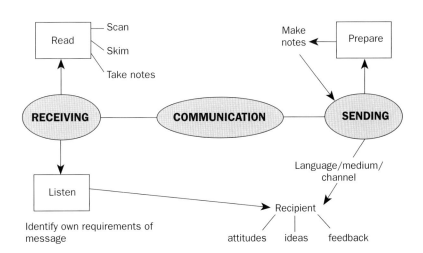

Figure 31 Simple diagrammatic notes

Organisational culture   The culture of an organisation can be defined as the relationship between the members and the way in which the organisation operates. Consider the implications of Figure 32, which shows different elements of a corporate culture.

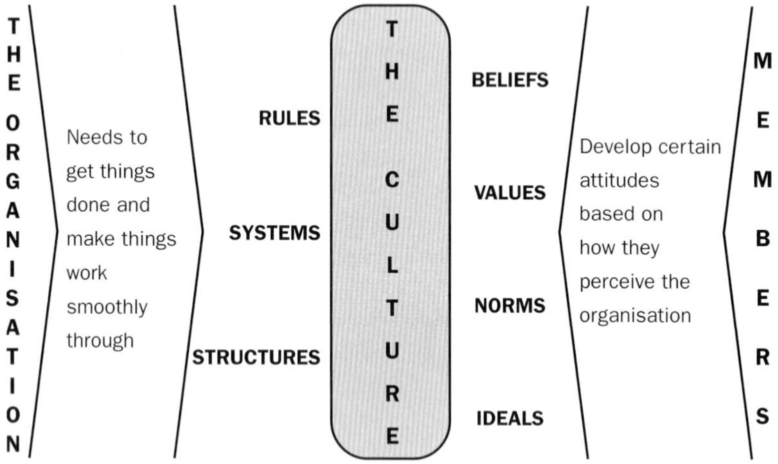
THE ORGANISATION
Needs to get things done and make things work smoothly through
RULES
SYSTEMS
STRUCTURES
THE CULTURE
BELIEFS
VALUES
NORMS
IDEALS
Develop certain attitudes based on how they perceive the organisation
MEMBERS

Figure 32 The culture of an organisation

The interrelationship and reinforcement of these concepts through 'normal' organisational activities establishes the overall culture. Obviously different organisations develop different cultures, and we can identify four main classifications, each of which have their individual characteristics and can be related to 'types' of organisation (Figure 33).

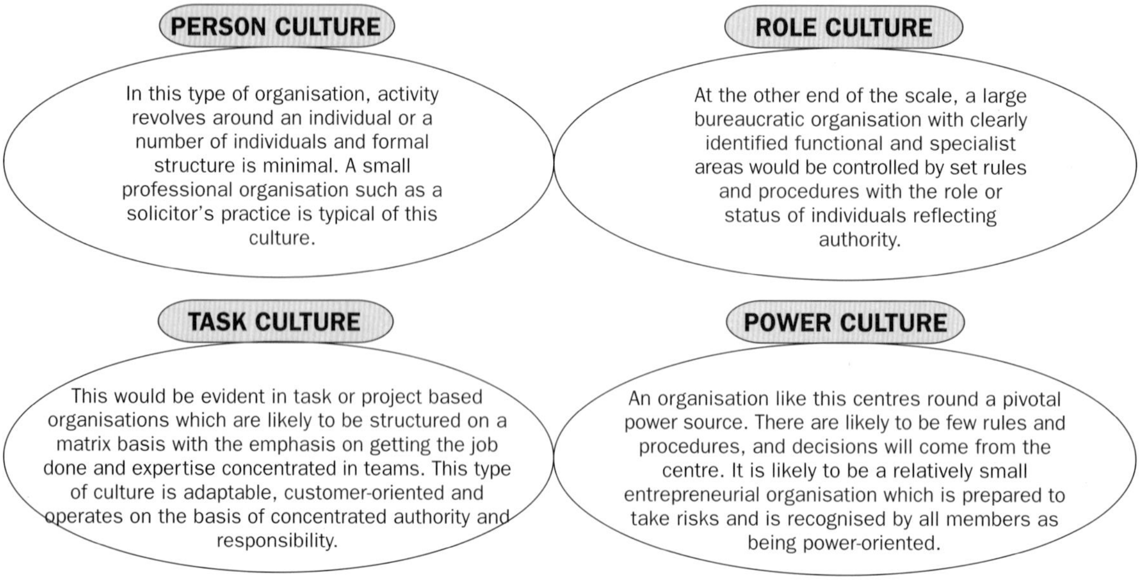
PERSON CULTURE
In this type of organisation, activity revolves around an individual or a number of individuals and formal structure is minimal. A small professional organisation such as a solicitor's practice is typical of this culture.
ROLE CULTURE
At the other end of the scale, a large bureaucratic organisation with clearly identified functional and specialist areas would be controlled by set rules and procedures with the role or status of individuals reflecting authority.
TASK CULTURE
This would be evident in task or project based organisations which are likely to be structured on a matrix basis with the emphasis on getting the job done and expertise concentrated in teams. This type of culture is adaptable, customer-oriented and operates on the basis of concentrated authority and responsibility.
POWER CULTURE
An organisation like this centres round a pivotal power source. There are likely to be few rules and procedures, and decisions will come from the centre. It is likely to be a relatively small entrepreneurial organisation which is prepared to take risks and is recognised by all members as being power-oriented.

Figure 33 Different elements of a corporate culture

Activity 15

Write a short commentary on your own organisation, or one with which you are familiar, describing the *culture* that predominates.

You will need to outline the type of organisation and its structure first of all, and then explain how the culture manifests itself in everyday activities, procedures, processes and relationships. Your submission should be no longer than two sides of A4 paper.

Unit 13

Motivation, the individual and the group

Most people regard themselves as individuals first, and after that as members of particular human groups (eg family, work group, social group, etc), some of the groups changing regularly according to current interests and occupations.

In this unit we are concerned with the individual at work, and how groups can affect the working environment. Most people go to work for a number of reasons, ranging from satisfaction of basic needs to fulfilment of personal ambitions and achievement of 'wants'. The interaction of these driving forces is complex, but determines each person's attitude and approach to working as part of an organisation.

Motivation theory

How many of the motivating factors listed here would you associate with your own approach to work?

satisfaction	friendship	somewhere to live
security	challenge	authority
food	status	creativity
protection from 'want'	pride	power
ambition	clothes	providing for family
improved standard of living	self-expression	'belonging'
using skills	economic	self-improvement

Activity 16

The motivating factors above can be classified into three main groups: primary, social and personal.

Task 1 Write a brief definition of what you understand by these terms – that is, what they mean to you (max. 5–8 lines each).

Task 2 Draw up a table, and classify the motivating factors listed above under one of the three group headings.

Note: The purpose of this activity is to help you think about the general concept of motivation from a personal point of view, and recognise that it does exist in many forms for all of us. The relative importance of individual factors will change for each individual, as we all have different needs, wants and priorities.

These motivating factors, and others, have been discussed, analysed and explained by management theorists for many years, and one of the main reasons for devoting so much time and talent to this sort of study is a perceived benefit in establishing a universal 'Theory of Management' which would enable all business organisations to be managed in an efficient and effective manner. However, this 'ideal' situation is unlikely to be achieved as long as organisations are made up of a collection of individuals, because everyone reacts differently to different stimuli, and (as we discussed earlier) an effective management style needs to be flexible and constantly adapted.

Many ideas put forward by the theorists are valid as ideas, but don't necessarily stand up to analysis when applied to real business situations; and it is generally accepted that there has been a lack of uniformity of study methods, and even some confusion over what 'management' is! Contributors to the management debate have come from a variety of backgrounds, including practising managers, sociologists, psychologists, industrial psychologists, mathematicians, organisation theorists and even biologists. It is no wonder that ideas differ and theories abound.

Despite the confusing background to the science of management, it is useful to have an awareness of some of the 'big names' in management thought, and, in the context of our studies, some knowledge of their ideas on *motivation*.

In his essay, 'The Motivational Basis of Organisational Behaviour' (1964), D. Katz said that an organisation could only function properly and effectively if the following three types of behaviour could be identified:

1 People must be induced to enter and remain within the system. High labour turnover and excessive absenteeism adversely affect the functioning of the organisation, but the mere fact that people attend work is not enough.

2 People must perform their appointed jobs in a dependable fashion, because if an organisation is to function at all there must be an ongoing, stable pattern of activities and relationships.

3 In addition to the basic requirements 1 and 2, people must at times (assuming that the job allows it) demonstrate initiative, spontaneous activity and innovative approaches to achieving organisational objectives above and beyond that which is normally expected of them.

Most people would accept these points at face value as they establish a basis for organisational operation, but within this framework a whole range of motivation theory can be considered.

We shall concentrate on a summary of the ideas of four main theorists who provide some interesting ideas on motivation, and who are recognised as having made a substantial contribution to the development of modern thought and work practice.

Chris Argyris

An American, with a background in psychology, Argyris looks at the impact of an organisation on the individual, and criticises the formal business organisation from the point of view that its objectives are automatically in conflict with those of individual employees. He maintains that every individual has undeveloped potential, which, given the right environment and conditions, can be brought to fulfilment. Formal organisation, with its chain of command, spans of control, emphasis on 'instruction', and high degree of specialisation requiring minimum skill and thought levels, restricts personal and individual development, and creates a dependent, subordinate work culture where initiative and innovative thought have no place.

Obviously, something has to give. Frustration can build up, a feeling of failure is common, and conflict can occur. Within the workforce certain behavioural patterns might be identified: eg high turnover of staff; apathy and disinterest; unprovoked aggression; a tendency to daydream; increased evidence of errors; restricted practices; emphasis on wanting 'more money'.

A typical reaction to this from the management of a formal organisation is a move towards a more autocratic, directive approach, an increase in controls and less opportunity for individual expression or development. Costs are likely to rise as output drops, mistakes multiply and management resort to 'bribery' to maintain appropriate work levels (eg 'bonuses', improved social and welfare facilities, etc).

Argyris's hypotheses provide some useful basic ideas for us to think around, and his solutions are quite easy to accept:

- Aim at the full development of individual potential.

- Involve workers in consultation and even in decision-making procedures.

- Give scope for free expression of ideas and feelings.

- Look at the actual jobs to see how they can be 'enlarged'.

Note: We look more closely at 'the job' in the next unit.

Abraham Maslow   Another psychologist by background, Maslow has looked at motivation in a very broad sense, starting with the question, 'Why do people work at all?' His underlying assumption in thinking about this is that every human being has needs, ranging from basic psychological needs to 'higher-level' needs. He thus gives us his *hierarchy of human needs* (Figure 34).

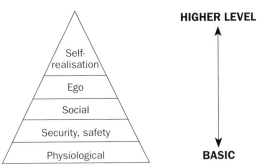

Figure 34 Maslow's hierarchy of human needs

Let's consider what he means by each of these needs, and try to identify with each 'level' as it applies to our own feelings/experience/situation.

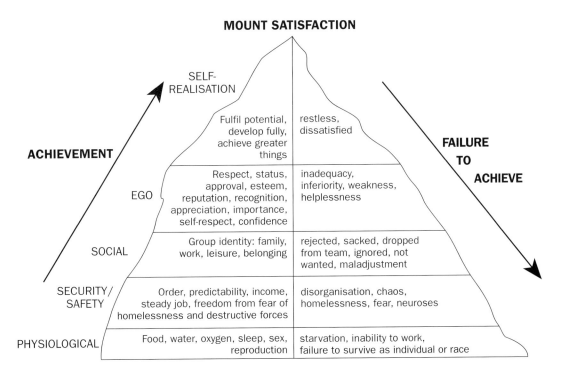

Figure 35 Maslow's hierarchy applied to personal feelings

Maslow's argument is that as soon as one need is satisfied, another group of needs emerge, and so it goes on. Therefore, it is only unsatisfied needs that motivate people to do things. On the negative side, the 'mountain' diagram (Figure 35) also indicates some possible effects of an individual's failure to satisfy/achieve his or her needs.

Maslow himself qualifies his own theories:

- There are creative people who are motivated by the self-actualisation need, despite the fact that other needs are *not* satisfied.

- People may have very low levels of aspiration, if their life experience has been narrow. A starving peasant may be satisfied for the rest of his life if he suddenly gets food regularly.

- Satisfied needs lead to new wants, as we have seen. The new wants continue even when the lower needs suddenly become unsatisfied. The unemployed director may still go to expensive concerts or go to the golf club even though he has no money coming in and is practising (for him) incredible economies in other directions.

- Further to the last point, some people have ideals, religious views or values, which they will maintain against public opinion, the state and armed force. With such values, people will become martyrs. The need to maintain their values outweighs any other need.

Douglas McGregor

McGregor's background as a social scientist, and his own experiences in managerial and executive positions, led to the development of his famous 'X' and 'Y' theories as the basis of his analysis of the behaviour of people at work. Some people think he used two extreme points of view to demonstrate particular aspects of his theories. See what you think!

His 'X' theory outlines a historical perspective in terms of traditional management attitudes, which he implies revolved around control, discipline, conformity, obedience and dependence. The essential theory can be summarised as follows:

- The average human being has an inherent dislike of work, and will avoid it if he/she can.

- Because of this human characteristic dislike of work, most people must be coerced, controlled, directed, threatened with punishment to get them to put forth adequate effort toward the achievement of organisational objectives.

- The average human being prefers to be directed, wishes to avoid responsibility, has relatively little ambition and wants security above all.

Actual thought about this will lead us to realise that if you treat people as if they are stupid, troublesome, inferior beings, they will either end up believing that they are all these things, or there is likely to be some adverse reaction or even rebellion. If they rebel, the theory 'X' manager immediately identifies the need for more control, more discipline – creating a vicious circle of conflict and repression and reinforcing already polarised attitudes.

Theory 'Y' shows the other extreme, and can be seen as a foundation for what we might now call 'participative management'. The following set of statements summarises McGregor's ideas:

- The expenditure of physical and mental effort in work is as natural as play or rest.

- External control and the threat of punishment are not the only means of bringing about effort toward organisational objectives. People will work, and discipline themselves to work towards objectives to which they are committed.

- People's commitment to objectives is in proportion to the rewards associated with achieving the objectives. (These rewards could be the satisfaction of ego and self-actualisation needs.)

- The average person learns, under proper conditions, not only to accept but also to seek responsibility.

- The ability to apply a relatively high degree of imagination, ingenuity and creativity to the solution of organisational problems is widely, not narrowly, distributed in the population.

- Under the conditions of modern industrial life, the intellectual potential of the average person is only partially fulfilled.

Obviously it is not easy to implement an organisational plan to facilitate all this, but some recognised approaches are shown in Figure 36.

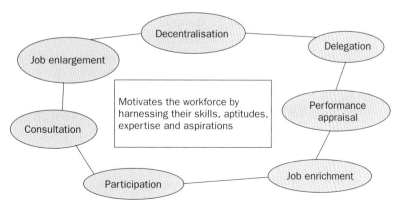

Figure 36 Organisational plan incorporating McGregor's theories

Frederick Herzberg

Herzberg was the proponent of the *Motivation – Hygiene Theory* which closely links the ideas of job satisfaction and motivation. The essence of his original research was that people related their ideas of what was good or bad about their jobs to completely different aspects of human nature – see Figure 37.

Figure 37 Herzberg's 'Motivation – Hygiene' theory

Therefore the concept of satisfaction seemed to be related to the quality of the job – job content – which facilitated personal growth and development. These became motivating factors which encouraged individuals to put more effort into what they were doing in order to gain more satisfaction. The 'hygiene' element of the theory relates to the concept of 'working conditions', and we should take this phrase in its broadest sense to mean not only physical conditions, but all the constraints and limitations under which people work. Herzberg maintained that constant monitoring and adjustment of the 'hygiene' factors, while not creating job satisfaction, can go a long way towards counteracting dissatisfaction. If the 'hygiene' factors are right, conditions are then conducive to motivating employees through improving the job – ie *enrichment* – to incorporate a wider range of skills and greater opportunity for personal development/growth.

Activity 17 This activity is in two parts. You will only be able to complete Task 2 if you have access to reasonable research facilities such as an academic or good public library.

Task 1 Using your reading in this unit as the basis for your observations, identify and explain aspects of the theories of Argyris, Maslow, McGregor and Herzberg that seem to overlap, support or agree with each other. You can support your suggestions by further reading and research if facilities are available to you.

Task 2 Research the ideas of other motivational theorists, and identify any principles or approaches that you can relate to the basic theories summarised in this text. As this is a very broad field, you should aim to discuss no more than three related concepts, making sure that you identify the 'author' (the theorist), explain concisely which aspect of his/her theories you are dealing with, and show how this theory links with the ideas of one or more of the theorists we have considered.

To help you get started on your research, here are some names to consider:

Max Weber
Henri Fayol
Elton Mayo
Rensin Likert
E. F. Schumacher
Frederick Taylor

Unit 14

Motivation and the job

In the previous units of this section you have been introduced to some ideas and activities relating to a range of business concepts which affect the performance of a job, including motivation, management styles, group dynamics, appraisal systems and change. Now we must look at the job itself. As we have seen, workers' perception of their jobs will influence their attitudes and behaviour. If a job is interesting, varied, and gives the performer a degree of responsibility and autonomy, the results can be very different, encouraging a conscientious and committed approach to work. The design of a job is therefore very important and the implementation of ideas such as job rotation, job enlargement and job enrichment can move some way towards creating a feeling of job satisfaction.

In many working situations the main criterion for job design has usually been to minimise the immediate costs of performing the operation and increase productivity, with little consideration being given to the needs of the individual worker. It's no wonder that some organisations suffer from high absenteeism, high turnover of staff and consequent increases in operational costs. Obviously, it is good business practice to cut costs and increase output, but one of the bases for achieving this should ideally be through a better motivated and more satisfied workforce.

When change is necessary

The most difficult task for any organisation is to identify when changes are necessary, and it is a function of management to be sensitive to the tell-tale signs that things are not entirely satisfactory on the shop-floor, amongst the administrative staff, or even amongst supervisory staff and middle management. Regular consultation with employees and union representatives will usually reveal any undercurrents of dissatisfaction, but there may also be more general problems which point to the need for change and often precede a 'droop' in the overall performance of the organisation (Figure 38).

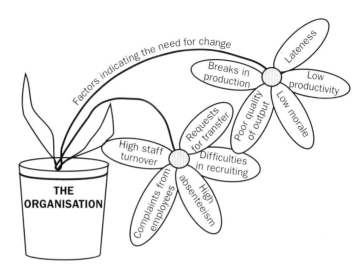

Figure 38 Symptoms of 'droop' in a company's performance

When the need for change has been identified, there are certain principles that need to be borne in mind if any attempt to re-design or restructure work is to be made. These revolve around the ideal requirements of a well-designed job. Obviously, there are considerations relating to the general work environment (eg physical factors such as heating, lighting, decor, atmosphere, noise, etc) and the interrelationship of work groups, sections and departments, but the job itself is a primary influence on the individual worker, and in a perfect situation should have as many of the characteristics shown in Figure 39 as possible.

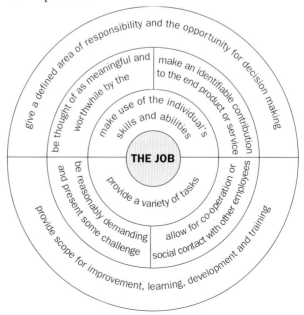

Figure 39 Characteristics of a job which should be considered in any plan for change

Job rotation   One of the most common methods of giving employees more variety in work activity, and at the same time expanding the range of knowledge and skills they can offer, is job rotation. This 'job swapping' can bring a greater understanding of the range of operations in which an organisation is involved, and help employees recognise the importance of their own job in the sequence of activities. From the company's point of view, other advantages are that the flexibility of the workforce is increased and a more efficient utilisation of staff is possible.

Despite the apparent benefits, job rotation has its limitations, because the basic level of work in which the employee is engaged remains the same, and there are difficulties in the implementation where any 'demarcation' situation exists. Because of this, job rotation should be introduced with great care and forethought, after adequate consultation with the individuals concerned and with union representatives.

Job enlargement   Another way of increasing interest and involvement is through job enlargement. Sometimes referred to as 'horizontal job-building', it involves expanding the scope of duties for which one person is responsible. In one sense, it is the opposite of extreme specialisation (eg where one clerk is responsible for opening letters; another extracts the contents; another identifies the recipient; and a fourth puts the contents into the appropriate tray). Such enlargement encourages staff to perform a range of activities related to their main job and, hopefully, avoids the boredom of constantly repeating the same task, and increases satisfaction by giving the employee more awareness of, and responsibility for, a broader span of achievement.

Job enrichment   Whereas job enlargement is a horizontal broadening process, job enrichment can be regarded as a vertical expansion of an individual's responsibilities. It need not necessarily involve an increase in the number of tasks an individual has to perform, but it does aim to involve the employee in decision-making and consultative processes, as well as introducing the principle of accountability. Such a development could mean the removal of constant supervisory control, more freedom in work practices, involvement in more complex procedures, more regular assessment/appraisal/review meetings, and more employee involvement in target setting, establishing objectives, and objective reviews of performance.

Activity 18 You should be able to complete this activity if you are currently employed in a full-time or part-time job, or if you have access to someone who is willing to discuss their job in detail, including the tasks involved and the way in which their organisation works. Whichever of these situations you can iden-tify with, the first task is to establish the main purpose of the job, and then suggest ways in which the work situation could be improved by job enlarge-ment and job enrichment. The results of this activity can be presented as a commentary and a chart, and may be used as a basis for in-class discussion to determine the extent to which these concepts can be applied to different types of job and real work situations.

The format in Figure 40 gives an indication of how your information can be structured, and guidelines are incorporated to give you some idea of contents.

Job Title ....

Main purpose of job
This should outline the main aim of the job and how it fits into the sequence of activities in the section/department/organisation.

Role of Supervisor/Section Head/Senior
What is he/she responsible for? What direct contact is there with the job holder? Who decides who shall do what? To whom is he/she responsible?

Extent of discussion/consultation between job holder and Supervisor/Section Head/Senior
Daily instructions? Direct supervision? Checking of work? Regular appraisal? Informal chats? Formal con-sultation/planning?

Required contact with others
Outline the extent to which co-operation with other staff, or reliance on other staff, affects the performance of the tasks involved in the job. For example, do you have to work in conjunction with someone else? Do you have to consult a Supervisor/Section Head/Senior? Is someone else waiting for your work to be passed on to them? etc.

THE JOB
Main tasks
Specify the range of tasks involved: _____

Ways in which the job could be enlarged

Suggest ways in which the job could be made more satisfying by incorporating a wider range of activities so that, for example, the job holder could complete a whole process rather than one part of it. Could the number of tasks be reduced, but the breadth of content increased? Make spe-cific suggestions.

Ways in which the job could be enriched

Remember that 'enrichment' is vertical expan-sion, increasing responsibility and accountability, and involving the job holder in the decision-making process. Can you see how this can be done with the particular job you are analysing here?

Figure 40
Assessing the scope for change in a job

Unit 15

Monitoring and quality control

One element of motivation and satisfaction for individuals at work is to know they are doing a good job, that the product or service they are delivering is of the highest quality to meet customer needs.

The monitoring and control of quality is a central management activity, and reference has already been made to this concept in Section One where one of the case studies introduced you to the idea of total quality management (TQM), and in Unit 8, Section Two, dealing with teams and teamwork. Figure 41 shows how management activity can be applied to this process.

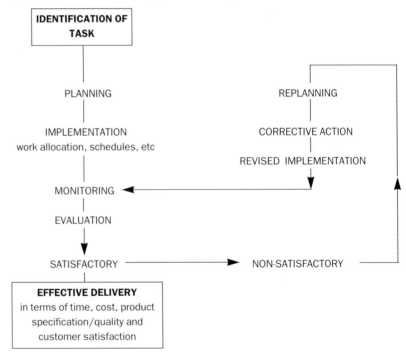

Figure 41 The application of management activity to the monitoring and control of quality

It is obvious that the main determinant for almost any product is the market: customers will react favourably to consistent availability, competitive price, high quality and effective service, and unfavourably to any negative experiences including late delivery or product unreliability. Management has to perform a balancing act, maximising all aspects of quality and minimising costs.

Let's consider some implications of 'total quality', and look first of all at the product (Figure 42).

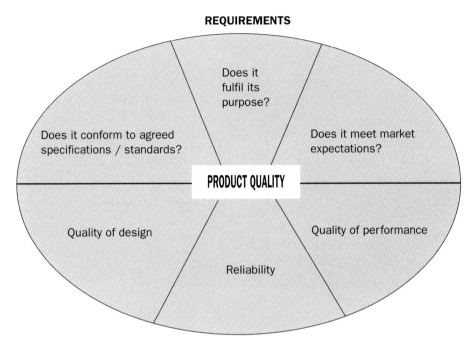

Figure 42 Aspects of product quality

At the production stage, or – in the case of a service – during performance, a quality control policy is adopted by many organisations which essentially means that unsatisfactory 'outcomes' are rejected. This can be quite an expensive business as in addition to initial production costs there have to be added the failure costs, inspection costs, rectification costs and the loss of customer goodwill. All these have to be carefully monitored and balanced so that an optimum quality level is identified.

However, 'total quality management' is not just the responsibility of management – *all* personnel and functional areas need to be committed to the concept, and work towards the overall organisational aims. A variety of activities and mechanisms can encourage this approach and provide monitoring/evaluation opportunities, but it can be a hard climb to success (Figure 43).

A number of quality controls can be monitored by computer

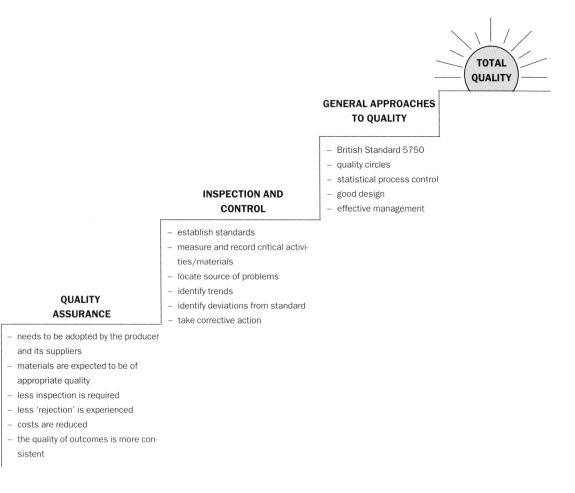

Figure 43 The climb to success in total quality management

Assessment Six   This assessment is in two parts, the first concentrating on *motivation* and the second on *quality*.

Task 1   You have had plenty of opportunity in this section to think about and investigate a range of ideas relating to organisational structure, motivation, job design and the behaviour of people at work. In this final assessment you will need to draw on a range of skills and a broad span of knowledge in order to collect, collate and present the information required.

   The aim of the assessment is to conduct a survey to *identify and rank motivating factors at work*. Your research should be based upon a particular group of people in a named organisation, and the findings will be presented in a formal report submitted to the Personnel Director. Your role is that of Consultant Research Assistant. You will need to complete the following activities.

1   Identify your organisation.

2   Briefly describe its structure and main function(s).

3   Identify the 'sample' on which your research is based (ie how many people, which department(s), what status).

4   Draw an organisation chart to show where your sample(s) fits in to the overall structure.

5   Construct a questionnaire. (See Figures 45 and 46 on pages 119–120 for help with this.)

6   Conduct the research.

7   Analyse the findings.

8   Present the findings in a formal report with appropriate evidence, and a conclusion that comments on the impact of motivating factors on personal performance.

Remember the aim: to *identify* and *rank*.

■   You can select any organisation of which you have experience, or to which you can gain access, but it should be a work organisation rather than one that is social, sporting or voluntary.

■   As your survey relates to a specific organisation, the sample can be relatively small. Discuss this with your tutor if you have any doubts. Obviously, the larger the sample, the more credible the results.

■   It could be easier if you limit your survey to one identified group or level in the organisation, in order to give comparability. However, the structure of your sample should be discussed and agreed with your tutor.

■   An outline structure for the report is given in Figure 44 on page 118.

■   You can enlist the help of anybody who can give you access to the required information for this assignment. If you are employed, use your own organisation and persuade your colleagues to help you with the questionnaire. If you are not currently employed, you will certainly know someone (friend or family) who will be able to give you the necessary information, and be willing to circulate a few questionnaires at their place of work. Full-time students can use any organisation to which they can get access, or base research on their college/department.

Note: You should revise the requirements and structure of a short formal report – see page 28.

For the attention of ....

Report on a survey of motivating factors in ....

1   TERMS OF REFERENCE

2   PROCEDURE

3   LIMITATIONS OF SURVEY

4   THE ORGANISATION
     (a) *Description*
     (b) *Structure*
     (c) *Main activities*

5   THE SAMPLE
     (a) *Size*
     (b) *Composition* (age, sex, functional area, status/position, etc)

6   THE QUESTIONNAIRE (how it was structured and why)

7   ANALYSIS AND COMMENTARY ON RESULTS
     This is the main section in which you should aim to identify personal
     attitudes, and *rank* motivating factors. Visual presentation of data will
     be given credit, eg bar charts, graphs, pie-charts.

8   CONCLUSIONS
     This section should be used to comment upon the impact of identified
     motivating factors on personal performance.

                                    Signature: ....

                                    Designation: ....

                                    Date: ....

Figure 44 Possible structure for a survey report

Task 2   Your organisation has been adopting a positive 'quality' policy for some time, and there has been some talk of applying for BS 5750. Nobody is too sure of what is involved, and when you indicate that you have at least heard of it, you are 'pounced' upon as the ideal person to do some research.

You are asked to find out as much as you can about the certification process and the implications for the organisation, and submit the information in a memo to a senior manager (you should decide which one is appropriate). Your memo should include information on the following aspects:

■   What is BS 5750?

■   What are its aims?

■   How does it operate?

■   What procedures have to be followed?

■   What are the implications for the organisation?

- How is certification achieved?

- What are the benefits for the organisation?

Surveys and questionnaires –
some basic guidelines

Surveys are generally regarded as being an integral part of market research, and used as part of the process of investigating a new market – its size, potential for growth, ability to generate profit, the competition and the customers.

However, the survey can also be a useful method of monitoring and investigating in-house operations and identifying people's reactions/feelings about what is going on in an organisation. The main tool of this type of survey is the questionnaire, and obviously the essential elements of the questionnaire are the questions.

It is not an easy task to draft and structure a questionnaire so that it is effective and user-friendly. However, the guidelines presented in Figures 45 and 46 should help you to establish an acceptable approach.

T	■ Should be easily understood	*avoid technical or complex language*
H	■ Should require a precise answer	*'yes', 'no', a date, a number, a place, a measurement, a fact*
E	■ Should not be ambiguous	*there should be no chance of misinterpretation or double meaning*
Q	■ Should use precise language	*words of vague meaning should be avoided eg what is large or small to one person will be different for another person*
U		
E		
S	■ Should not demonstrate bias	*no leading questions; no emotive language; nothing that will cause offence; nothing indicating a required answer*
T		
I	■ Should not require calculations to be made	*too time-consuming and prone to error*
O		
N	■ Should not ask the correspondent to classify information	*can lead to too many 'don't knows'*
S	■ Should use a variety of question types	*eg open, closed, prioritising, scaled*

Figure 45 The essentials of good questionnaire design

THE CLOSED QUESTION

Requires a single response – often yes/no.

| Do you smoke? | Yes ☐ | No ☐ |
| Do you own a car? | Yes ☐ | No ☐ |

THE OPEN QUESTION

Requires a personalised response – and a longer answer. Not suitable for numerical/percentage analysis.

How are you affected by fluorescent light?
What do you like about this particular colour scheme?

THE SCALED QUESTION

Respondents have a limited choice of graded answers. Useful for statistical analysis.

How would you assess the counselling and guidance you received before the course?

Very good ☐   Fairly good ☐   Adequate ☐   Not very good ☐   Poor ☐

THE PRIORITISING QUESTION

Designed to rank preferences – good for numerical analysis.

Place the following features in order of importance,
where 1 is the most important and 7 the least important.

Electric sun-roof	☐
Heated seat pads	☐
Central locking system	☐
Electric windows	☐
Portable/detachable radio-cassette	☐
Adjustable steering wheel	☐
Electronic alarm	☐

Figure 46 Types of question

Appendix

Coverage of elements and performance criteria

Each activity and assessment in this text contributes towards achievement of the elements and performance criteria indicated here.

Activity/Assessment	GNVQ Advanced
Activity 1	15.1.1, 15.1.2, 15.3.1
Activity 2	15.1.1, 15.1.2
Assessment One	15.1.2, 15.1.3, 15.2.3, 15.2.4, 15.3.3, 15.3.4
Assessment Two	15.1.1, 15.1.2, 15.1.3, 15.2.4, 15.3.1, 15.3.2, 15.3.4
Activity 3	15.2.1, 15.2.2, 15.2.3
Activity 4	15.2.1, 15.2.2, 15.2.3
Assessment Three	15.1.1, 15.1.2, 15.2.2, 15.2.3
Activity 5	15.1.2, 15.1.3
Activity 6	15.1.1, 15.1.2, 15.2.2, 15.2.3, 15.2.4, 15.3.2
Assessment Four	15.1.1, 15.1.2, 15.2.4
Activity 7	15.1.1, 15.1.2, 15.1.3, 15.3.3
Activity 8	15.1.1, 15.2.2, 15.2.4, 15.3.1, 15.3.2, 15.3.3, 15.3.4
Assessment Five	15.1.1, 15.1.2, 15.2.4, 15.3.1, 15.3.2
Activity 9	15.1.1, 15.1.2, 15.3.4
Activity 10	15.3.3
Activity 11	15.3.3, 15.3.4
Activity 12	15.2.1, 15.2.3, 15.3.3
Activity 13	15.1.1, 15.1.2, 15.2.3
Activity 14	15.1.1, 15.1.2, 15.2.3
Activity 15	15.1.1, 15.1.2, 15.1.3
Activity 16	15.1.2
Activity 17	15.1.2, 15.2.4
Activity 18	15.1.1, 15.1.2, 15.1.3, 15.3.2
Assessment Six	15.1.1, 15.1.2, 15.1.3, 15.3.2

Index